DAVID TAYLOR'S
KINGDOM
OF
ANIMALS

PIPIT
PRESS

Acknowledgements

The publishers would like to thank the following for permission to reproduce photographs in this book:

Bruce Coleman Limited: pages, 11, 17, 60, 146, right (Rod Williams); 12 (WWF/Paul Trummer); 15, 131, 151 (Bruce Coleman); 18, 19, 54, top left, 101 (Jane Burton); 21, 28, 59, left, 170 (Norman Myers); 22, 141, 173, 174 (John Cancalosi); 23, 54, bottom right, 55, 84, 91, 105, bottom, 138 (Jeff Foott); 24 (Alan Root); 26, 162 (J.L.G. Grande), 27, 97, 99, 152 (Jen and Des Bartlett), 29 (Allan Power); 31 (Andy Purcell); 32 (Jon Kenfield); 33 (Neville Coleman); 35, 42 (Frieder Saner); 36 (Alfred Pasieka); 38, 104, 109, 110, 118, 122, 126 (Hans Reinhard); 43 (Peter Ward); 44 (Anthony Healy); 46 (David Hughes); 47, 48, 71, 96, bottom (Carol Hughes); 49 (M.P.L. Fogden); 58, 75, 128, 164 (Gerald Cubitt); 62 (Michael Freeman); 63, 66 (Simon Trevor); 65, 70, 80 (Gunter Ziesler); 67 (Len Rue Junior); 68, 72 (Masood Quraishy); 74 (Alain Compost); 76 (F. Vollmar); 78 (Frans Lanting); 81 (WWF/Al Giddings); 89, 147 (Mark Boulton); 90 (John M. Burnley); 103 (Francisco Erize); 105, top (Ken Balcomb); 106 (Kim Taylor); 111, 130, 133 (Charles Hennighein); 115 (Fritz Prenzel); 116 (Eric Crichton); 127 (Leonard Lee Rue 111); 137, 145 (L.C. Marigo); 139 (WWF/ H. Jungius); 140 (Sullivan and Rogers); 149, 168 (Christian Zuber); 155, right (C.B. and D.W. Frith); 159 (John Wallis); 161 (John Visser); 163 (John Topham); 165 (Stephen J. Krasemann); 169 (Rod Williams); 175 (John Anthony). Oxford Scientific Films Limited: pages 13, 39 (J.A.L. Cooke); 40 (Babs and Bert Wells); 87 (Pam and Willy Kemp); 142 and 146, left. Heather Angel: page 83. The Hulton Picture Library; pages 108 and 113. The Imperial War Museum: pages 96, top; 119, 121; 125; 132. The Mansell Collection Ltd: page 117. Ardea London Ltd: pages 148 and 156.

Published in Great Britain by Pipit Press in 1990.
Pipit Press is an imprint of Boxtree Limited,
36 Tavistock Street, London WC2E 7PB

Text © David Taylor 1990
Artwork © Boxtree Limited 1990
Illustrated by David Quinn
Designed by Groom & Pickerill

Abbreviations	
mm	millimetre
cm	centimetre
m	metre
km	kilometre
kmh	kilometres per hour
ha	hectare
gm	gram
kg	kilogram

CONTENTS

Introduction

*D*uring the long march of evolution, millions of species of animal, large and small, have vanished for ever. The creatures that share the Earth with us today – over 2 million different species – exist because their ancestors, and they themselves, have successfully, brilliantly adapted to a role in a world which is unceasingly, ever so slowly, changing. All living animals, in short, have shown the ability to cope. Only arrogant modern man with his technology threatens to exterminate thousands of species which have taken millions upon millions of years to become, in all their perfection, what they are today.

With the glittering variety of the animal kingdom some creatures survive by sheer power and strength, while others use highly specialised means of defending themselves or obtaining food – the 'poisoners' are among the most fascinating of these. Some have struck up a close relationship with man through domestication and this has led to them being exploited by the perennial human thirst for conflict and war: unwittingly, unwillingly, animals have been dragooned into serving as battle animals. But there are many forms of exploitation and some animals suffer increasingly from human greed and carelessness. This latter group are the ones for whom the red light is flashing urgently, the ones who are most at risk of prematurely joining the Dodo and sabre-toothed tiger, never to be seen alive again – not because of the slow, *natural* process of evolution but because of *our* selfish ways. This book is about some of these animals, about how they survive and how they have survived – so far:

ANIMAL POISONERS

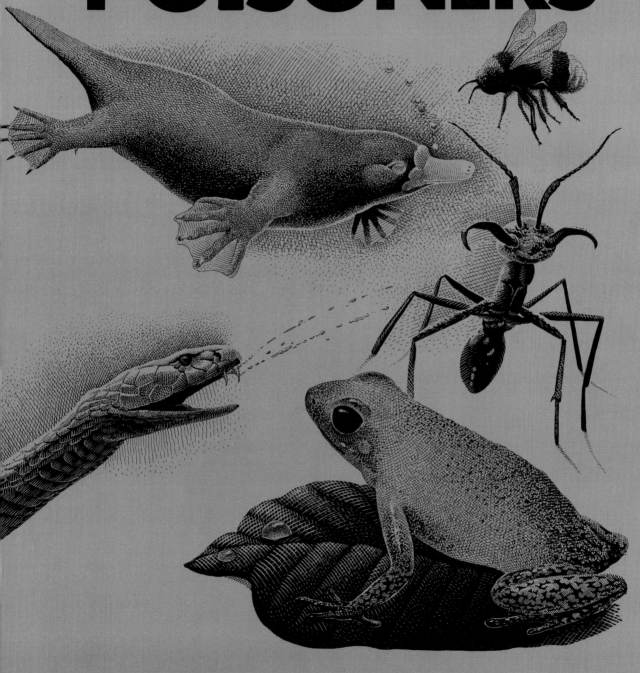

The old man was prospecting for gold among the rocks. It was nearly sundown and he took another swig of whisky from the bottle. His pick dislodged a small yellow boulder and something dark and squat, the length of his scrawny forearm, looked up at him with beady eyes. 'Hey! Look at you' said the old man out loud though there was no-one to hear him. The dark shape began to move away. 'Oh no ye don't!' exclaimed the old-timer throwing aside the pick and reaching down with bony fingers. He almost had the creature in his grip when, with surprising speed, the black head turned and its jaws clamped down on his thumb. Reeling from the shock and the whisky, the old man staggered back. The pain flared, but the *thing* wouldn't let go! He snatched at it with his other hand. It held on and clenched its jaws even tighter. The old prospector slumped against the rock face. His heart was pounding now and breathing seemed so difficult. Minutes later he lost consciousness . . . Before he died the *gila monster* detached itself and waddled silently away.

Venomous lizards

I have been to many places in the world where the inhabitants are firmly convinced that lizards are poisonous. Bedou in the deserts of the Arabian Peninsula swear the bite of the *agama*, a greenish-brown lizard, the male of which may possess a head of brilliant blue, is rich in venom. *Geckos*, those charming, fly-catching, gravity-defying lizards, that by

The thing wouldn't let go!

The dragon-like appearance of the gila monster.

night police the walls of houses in the Mediterranean, Africa and Asia, are considered venomous in some cultures.

In fact only one small family of lizards, out of over 3,000 known species of lizards, are venomous. That is the *Heloderma*. This family has two species: the *beaded lizard* and the gila (pronounced HEE-LAH) monster. Both have been given sinister Latin names by scientists: the beaded lizard is *Heloderma horridum* and the gila monster is *Heloderma suspectum*!

Fanciful folklore

As you might imagine with such an awesome name, the gila monster is the subject of much fanciful folklore in the areas they inhabit. Mexicans, for example, often call them *escorpion* – the Spanish name for scorpion. Perhaps some of the lizards' unwarranted evil reputation stems from injuries and deaths inflicted by real scorpions that live in the same habitat. It is said that the gila monsters' breath is poisonous, that they spit venom (like a spitting cobra), that they are magical creatures produced by crossing alligators and lizards, that they can bite large chunks out of people and other animals, and that they are immortal. All of this is nonsense.

Heloderms are actually shy, docile animals who never look for trouble. You would be extremely lucky to see one in the wild though they are exhibited (and thrive well) in the reptile houses of many zoological gardens.

They are sluggish, heavy-bodied creatures up to 80 cm in length with blunt heads, short limbs equipped with powerful digging claws, and a short, thick stumpy tail. The skin has a beady rather than scaly look and is marked with a 'Danger – I'm trouble' pattern, with alternating rings of blackish-brown and yellow or pinkish-orange.

The Heloderms aren't quick movers unless harassed or mishandled and they hunt 'easy' prey such as baby animals, nesting birds and eggs, employing their highly developed senses of smell and

> *They love not poison that do poison need.*
>
> Shakespeare *Richard II* (Act V, Sc. vi)

11

A gila monster relishes an egg for breakfast.

taste. They themselves lay eggs, hibernate during the winter, can swim very competently when necessary, and, quaintly, are said to sleep lying on their backs.

Most people who have been bitten by Heloderms have done something to provoke the lizard. A high percentage were drunks who teased the animals; others have handled them carelessly in zoos or laboratories. Heloderms just aren't aggressive; they like to keep clear of man and civilisation in general, and they don't strike in the same way as a snake, or leap to attack. Their rather blunt teeth cannot penetrate boots or shoes.

The agonising bite

Nevertheless the Heloderms are equipped with a powerful venom that affects the nervous system and can cause death through paralysis of the respiratory (breathing) muscles.

Unlike snakes who are fitted with venom glands in the *upper* jaw and hollow fangs that inject the poison, the Heloderms' venom glands are in the *lower* jaw and do not connect with the lizard's teeth. The Heloderm has several ducts situated in the gum between the lip and lower jaw bone to channel the venom from the glands, unlike the snake which has only one duct. The lizard's teeth are grooved and so when it bites a victim, the toxic juices flow along these grooves and into the victim. While snakes inject their venom, Heloderms chew and chomp it in.

As these lizards do not possess the very sophisticated poison-delivery system of the snake, they rely on their bulldog-like tenacity, holding on like grim death and working the venom into the flesh of the victim by chewing and tearing persistently. Nerve poisons of snakes are not normally painful when injected, but the bite of the Heloderm is agonising, firstly because of the chewing action and secondly because the venom also contains a chemical, *serotonin*, that produces pain.

Only about eight people are known to have died as a result of a gila monster or beaded lizard bite, and the majority of them were drunk or in poor health at the time. These fascinating and retiring creatures will cause us no harm if we treat them as we should all animals – with the utmost respect and kindness.

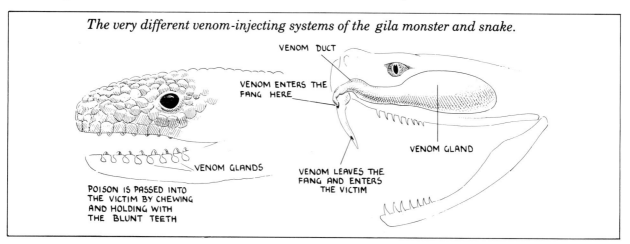

The very different venom-injecting systems of the gila monster and snake.

VENOM DUCT

VENOM ENTERS THE FANG HERE

VENOM GLAND

VENOM GLANDS

VENOM LEAVES THE FANG AND ENTERS THE VICTIM

POISON IS PASSED INTO THE VICTIM BY CHEWING AND HOLDING WITH THE BLUNT TEETH

The dragonfly nymph was about to make a kill. It clung with four of its six legs to a stem of waterweed. The clear stream water flowed silently around it. Half a metre above it, the water's surface glistened in the sunlight like a roof of silver silk. But the dragonfly nymph seemed unaware of the current's tug and the silver light above; its attention was fixed on the young frog sculling idly towards it. One more slow flick of those long hind legs, and the nymph would shoot out and seize the froglet with its hooked lower lips. Dinner was on its way!

A sudden shadow blocked out the sunlight, and even as it made its move towards the young frog, the nymph found itself snatched from its perch on the weed and drawn into darkness. As it felt itself crushed it caught a final brief glimpse of its attacker. It was a monster! Not a diving bird, not a rat, what could it be . . . ?

Real or fake?

Surely this must be a joke. Duck's bill, webbed and clawed feet, furry body, egg-laying but suckling its young on milk — could this be another of those fake animals so popular in Victorian museums constructed by skilfully stitching, say, the head of a fish to the body of a rabbit and the tail of a pheasant? Well, no. Those fraudulent and fantastic beasts were only to be found lifeless and stuffed in glass cases – whereas this animal *lives*. Most of us have never seen one. It is very rarely on view in zoos. What can it be? It is the *platypus*. And among its many remarkable features is the possession of venom, enough to cause severe pain and sickness in a human being or to kill a dog.

The famous, but little seen, *duck-billed platypus* is an Australian species, a member of the small group of animals called *Monotremes*, highly-specialised egg-laying mammals that are perhaps not as primitive as was once thought. The two other members of the group are the *short-beaked* and the *long-beaked echidna* – animals rather resembling hedgehogs though not related to them.

The platypus is a semi-aquatic, carnivorous individual up to 75 cm long and weighing 1-2.5 kg. It is perfectly designed for hunting worms and insect larvae which live at the bottom of freshwater rivers and streams. It is streamlined in shape with dense, waterproof fur covering

Not a hedgehog, but the platypus' distant relative the echidna, who also carries a spur, although a useless one.

The platypus searches for food underwater.

the body. It has fully-webbed fore feet that pull the animal through the water and partially-webbed hind feet that act as rudders. It keeps its eyes closed when swimming under water and uses its large flexible bill, which is packed with nerve endings, to probe for and locate its food. The adult platypus has no teeth (the youngsters have teeth but lose them when they emerge from the breeding burrows in late summer); instead it has cheek pouches lined with horny ridges for storing and grinding food.

In some places, particularly in winter, the habitat of the platypus can be very cold with temperatures that may drop below freezing. To cope with the cold the animal can turn up the heat produced by burning food within its body. At 32°C a platypus' normal body temperature is lower than most other animals except the South American sloth. In comparison, dogs' and cats' normal body temperature is 38-38.7°C. To help to keep it warm the platypus has the benefit of thick insulating fur and a snug burrow dug out in the river banks to retire to.

Platypus mums normally lay two eggs (sometimes one or three) and these hatch after about ten days. The eggs are laid in a special breeding burrow that is longer and more intricate than the normal 'home' burrow. Within the breeding burrows are one and sometimes more nursery chambers. The young platypuses stay in the burrow for three to four months feeding on the mother's milk which they suck from her belly fur near the openings of the mammary glands (breasts), which are really just specialised sweat glands. Unlike other mammals a female platypus has no nipples.

The snug riverbank burrow of a platypus can be up to 30m long.

About 100 years ago the platypus was almost extinct in many places, principally as a result of being hunted. Now, thank goodness, no-one is allowed to hunt it, and it has become quite common once more. Nevertheless it must be regarded as a vulnerable species whose numbers may soon begin to decline because of increasing threats by agriculture and industry to the freshwater habitat on which the platypus depends.

Poison spurs

But what about the poison, you ask! Where is the poison? In the duck-like bill? No, a platypus (and only a *male* platypus at that) produces the venom in a gland behind his knee and delivers it through a hollow, moveable, horny spur set on the ankle! This spur can be erected like flicking open a pen-knife blade, and then jabbed into something (or somebody) with a sharp kick of the hind legs. What use are the poison spurs of the platypus? We aren't sure. Perhaps they once served as a defensive weapon against some extinct

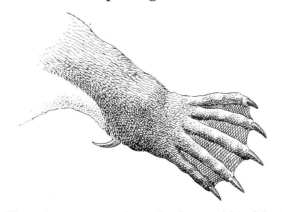

The poison spur on the male platypus' hind foot.

Oh what fun messing about in mud! A platypus hauls itself out of the water.

predator, but nowadays the creature has virtually no enemies except an occasional foraging dingo. Or perhaps it has something to do with finding a mate, for the poison glands get bigger during the breeding season. Whatever the reason, we can be sure that the platypus, a shy and retiring character, doesn't use the spurs for offensive purposes. If you were to pick up a male platypus, however, particularly during the breeding season, you might upset him and get a couple of spurs kicked into you. But such incidents are very rare indeed. Although people jabbed by platypus spurs have suffered great pain and puffy inflammation of the affected part for days, and sometimes weeks, there are luckily no lasting effects, and I know of no fatal cases.

So, this unlikely and intriguing creature is only a minor member of my list of animal poisoners and one who, once again, doesn't go looking for trouble but asks only to be left happily guddling about beneath the river's surface.

The farmer tapped his stick irritably on the ground. 'Today of all days,' he thought. 'Why did the accursed imp choose today?' The young grey horse stood a few metres away nodding slowly as if in agreement. The man flicked at it with his stick and the grey turned away and hobbled painfully out through the long grass. Lame – and on Michaelmas Day. The day of the great autumn fair at Dorchester. The fair to which he had planned to take the sack of walnuts and the flitch of bacon for Mistress Walpole. The fair where there would be a dancing bear and the pedlars of cloth, the blind piper and the casks of old ale. How now was he going to get to the fair? The horse was as lame as the crooked-legged cannoneer who had come home mangled after fighting for Cromwell, but who had somehow survived. The farmer watched the horse lie down.

He knew what had happened, of course. One of *them* had crept over it as it slept. Why, oh why, had he left it out in the meadow last night. *They* lived there and were well known to bring lameness to cattle and horses – even humans it was said, if you slept in the rick when haymaking was done.

Only one thing to do with the farrier still away at the wars. 'Ned!' he shouted to his son who was scything nearby. The boy must go and catch one of them, alive, and bury it in a hole he would bore in the ash

A fine little swimmer, the water shrew.

tree yonder. That would do it. The grey would no doubt be sound again in a day or two. But he would have to wait another year for the Michaelmas Fair.

Undeserved reputation?

The above scene is typical of old English country folks' superstitions about the cause and treatment of unaccountable lameness in animals and man, and such practices persisted in some parts of the country up to the end of the last century. It was believed that certain creatures could cause such an affliction simply by walking in front of a person or animal, in much the same way as people say, even today, that if a black cat crosses your path it will bring good luck. So the creature that the farmer sent his son to catch had an evil though undeserved reputation. What the farmer didn't know was that the animal he sought, though harmless to man and falsely accused of injuring his stock, was and *is* – for it is still common in the English countryside today – *venomous*. I am not, however, referring to the adder, Britain's only poisonous snake, but to the shrew which along with its relatives is the only group of venomous mammals apart from the duck-billed platypus.

Shrews are tiny mouse-like creatures with long, pointed noses; shy, secretive, solitary natures; and *very* bad tempers. They appear to be almost permanently annoyed, are seldom still, and yell and screech at the tops of their voices most of the time. The words 'shrew', 'shrewish',

'If you say I'm bad-tempered once again, you'll make me very cross!' A common tree shrew.

'shrewd', have for long been used in reference to people with certain characteristics associated with this bolshy little beast. I must admit that shrews don't seem to be the sort of folk one would like to meet!

There are about 250 different species of shrew scattered all over the world and they all have similar habits, though some are more aquatic than others. Apart from certain bats, the smallest living mammal is a shrew – *Savi's white-toothed pigmy shrew* of the Mediterranean coastline weighs a mere 1.5-2.5g. Shrews have the

shortest natural lifespan of all mammals – European common shrews rarely reach their first birthdays. Some shrews are very rare (*Hoy's pigmy shrew* is one of the rarest mammals in the USA) and some, like *Kelaart's long-clawed shrew* of the Sri Lankan mountains, have only been seen on a very few occasions since their original discovery.

Shrilling and twittering

Shrews communicate by touch and vocalisation – their high pitched shrilling and twittering, part of which is beyond the range of human ears, is one of their most characteristic features. Several shrew species including the *European common shrew* and the *European water shrew*, dig tunnel systems with nest chambers lined with grass or leaves where they can snatch a brief rest from their hectic lifestyles and rear their young. Aggressive and quarrelsome, they defend their territory vigorously and want nothing to do with any of their fellows except at mating time.

Shrews breed prodigiously with females giving birth to up to ten litters a year after pregnancies of 13-16 days. The newborn babies are fur-less and blind. When they are old enough to leave the nest they frequently form delightful 'caravans' by lining up one in front of the other, each gripping the bottom of the one in front and the leading youngster gripping Mum's rear. So tightly do they hold on that it is possible to pick up a shrew 'caravan' and dangle it (gently for a second or two) like a warm and furry chain.

Shrews are amazingly active and, with enormous appetites for bodies so small, are on the lookout for meals day and night. Because they can't store food for more than an hour or two in their bodies, they *must* eat virtually continually stopping only for short periods of sleep. They are mainly insectivorous and carnivorous (insect- and meat-eating), but some species will also feed on plant material such as nuts and seeds. Many set up food stores as an insurance against times of scarcity. Shrews have small, rather ineffective eyes, but wonderful senses of hearing and smell. They fuss and forage nervously in the undergrowth and leaf litter in search of worms, grubs, beetles and the like.

Water shrews have fringes of stiff hairs on their feet, toes and tail that help swimming and also trap air bubbles so that the lightweight animal can actually run across the surface of the water using the bubbles as floating shoes! Water shrews feed on small fish, froglets and other aquatic creatures using their venom to subdue the larger, stronger prey.

The venom of the shrew is produced in a pair of modified salivary glands whose ducts open near the base of the animal's four lower incisor teeth. The teeth jut forward and form a groove through which the poison can flow. The shrew doesn't produce much venom but it is effective in killing its prey. The *American short-tailed shrew* for example, has enough

venom to kill about 200 mice. The venom causes paralysis and convulsions in the shrew's prey with death following after a few minutes. The bite of a shrew is *not* dangerous to you and me, beyond the usual possibilities of local reaction, soreness and infection; there just isn't enough

'With a little bit of luck I'll find a tadpole somewhere down here.' A water shrew exploring its underwater world.

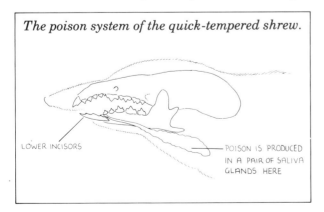

The poison system of the quick-tempered shrew.

LOWER INCISORS

POISON IS PRODUCED IN A PAIR OF SALIVA GLANDS HERE

power in the poison to do us any harm. Anyway, bites from shrews are very rare and deaths of human beings have never been reported.

As you walk through the countryside you may sometimes catch a glimpse of a shrew or find a dead one lying by the path. This tiny creature, foul-tempered and flustered though it may be, does no harm, and it certainly does not deserve its old reputation as a bearer of illness and bad luck. Burying a shrew alive in an ash tree to cure lameness was a cruel and useless superstition that has now, I am pleased to say, disappeared.

FRIGHTENING FANGS

s a zoo and wild animal vet, one of the commonest questions people ask me is: Which is the most dangerous animal that you work with? In the course of over 30 years' in my profession being doctor to Noah's Ark, I have treated killer whales with coughs, gorillas with toothache, grumpy tarantula spiders, tigers with tummyache, bears with boils, and sharks with swollen necks. During all that time my patients have inflicted remarkably few injuries upon me – a finger bitten to the bone by a monkey, an Achilles tendon hooked by the claws of a leopard, nothing serious.

It's lucky that this man is carrying a lantern. Otherwise he could easily have stepped on this threatening cobra, which was enjoying the day's warmth retained by the road stones.

Of course I treat all animals with respect and caution, and nowadays the zoo vet has a marvellous array of equipment and drugs, including blowpipes and flying darts, tranquilliser guns and special anaesthetics, to help him or her go about the daily business of healing safely.

What I have learned is that it isn't always the animals that you might expect to be the most dangerous that are. Lions, I find, aren't as fearsome as leopards, and an escaped adult chimpanzee causes far more havoc than a bull gorilla on the rampage. I have seen terrible injuries caused by aggressive zebras and eland antelopes, and many of the old big-game hunters of Africa claimed that *the* most dangerous creature to be found in that continent wasn't the lion, the crocodile *or* the rhinoceros, but the Cape buffalo. So

it's a difficult question for me to answer, but one animal that *I* am really frightened of, and thank goodness I only have to examine one perhaps two or three times a year, is none of these. Large, powerful, fast-moving, aggressive and deadly, it lives in the deep jungles of India and Burma and feeds on snakes. Its name? The *King cobra*.

A mouthful of venom

There are about 2,700 different species of snake alive today on earth and just over 400 (almost 15 per cent) are poisonous to man. It is extremely rare for the non-venomous constrictor snakes to kill a human being (I know of only about half a dozen authenticated cases), whereas venomous snakes kill between 30,000 and 40,000 people a year.

During the course of millions of years of evolution, venomous snakes have changed the main function and purpose of some of their saliva glands in the upper jaw. Saliva is normally a harmless liquid containing chemicals (enzymes) that aid

Beautiful but deadly – a green mamba searches for prey in birds' nests.

digestion. Snake venom still plays a role in digestion of the prey, but it now contains poisonous chemicals which immobilise and kill. It is interesting to note that there are snakes completely harmless to man which have just a little poison in their saliva. They show us how the change from non-venomous to venomous must have evolved.

Snake venom exists to help the animal first to get and then to digest its dinner. Defence is only a secondary purpose and the venom was certainly never intended for attacks on big animals like humans who could never form part of a snake's natural diet. The poison glands of the snake can be found either at the back or the front of the upper jaw. The venom leaves the gland through a duct and then runs down a groove on the outside of the fang or through a tube within the fang.

Snakes with grooved poison fangs at the back of the mouth ('back-fanged

With rattle a-rattling, a western diamondback rattlesnake adopts its typical threatening posture.

snakes') are not usually dangerous to man as they cannot open their mouths wide enough for the rear fangs to make contact with the body of such a large animal. There are exceptions among the larger back-fanged species – for example the dangerous *boomslang* of Africa. Snakes with poison fangs at the front of the mouth form the most lethal group from a human point of view. When the snake strikes the fangs are swung forward like flick-knife blades and the venom is injected into the victim by a jab rather than a bite. The venom is a mixture of chemicals with two principal constituents, the proportions of which vary according to the species of snake; one attacks the nervous system causing paralysis, and the other attacks the blood and circulatory system. Some snakes produce mainly the nerve-attacking poison, others the blood attacker, and others affect both systems in equal measure.

Nowadays antidotes called anti-venins, are available for the treatment of man (and domestic animals) bitten by snakes. To produce anti-venins it is necessary to 'milk' venom painlessly from a snake by holding it behind the head, opening its mouth and getting it to 'strike' by putting its fangs in contact with a rubber membrane stretched across the mouth of a glass beaker. Scientists study the complicated make-up of snake venoms in order to produce medicines which are of use in treating blood and other diseases of man and animals.

Top ten poisoners

Which are the most dangerous snakes in the world? Experts who have hunted, caught and studied snakes for many years may differ in their 'Top Ten' lists, though they would all agree with me on the 'Top Two'. Here is a list made by amalgamating the experts' personal choices.

1 King Cobra
2 Taipan
3 Mamba
4 Bushmaster
  Death adder
5 Tiger snake
  Western diamondback rattlesnake
6 Common cobra
  Fer-de-lance
7 Puff adder
  Tropical rattlesnake
8 Russell's viper
9 Saw-scaled viper
10 Jararacussa

The most famous venomous snake of North and South America is the *rattlesnake*, the only snake that has a true 'rattle' on the end of its tail to make the sinister noise so often heard in cowboy films. There are 66 different kinds of rattlesnake, some of them rare and confined to small areas. The species called the *Western diamondback* kills more people than any other snake in the USA, and even baby rattlers can deliver a lethal bite.

No coward

But to return to that most terrible of snakes, the King cobra. Luckily, and unlike some other cobras, the King cobra inhabits deep jungle and steers clear of human habitations. Although it is sometimes said that this snake will attack man on sight, I do not think that this is true. However, unlike all other snakes, it will not flee if it sees a human being approaching. The King cobra is no coward.

A King cobra, possibly the world's most dangerous snake, feeds on another snake.

A really dangerous snake: this spitting cobra aims its venom at the photographer's eyes.

Although I regard the King cobra as the most dangerous snake to tangle with, it is not the most venomous in terms of the strength of its poison. Sea snakes, adapted to life in warm oceans, possess venom 100 times more toxic than that of any other snake. Luckily they are relatively docile animals. Among land snakes the most powerful venom is manufactured by the *tiger snake* of Australia which can result in the death of humans untreated with anti-venin, in two to three hours.

One particularly tricky venomous snake is the *spitting cobra*, a species I find to be particularly bad-tempered and which can eject its venom out of its mouth with considerable accuracy. It usually aims for a person's eyes and can hit them quite easily from a distance of at least 2m to produce severe pain, temporary blindness and sometimes permanent injury. You can understand why I wear plastic goggles when working with spitting cobras!

THE STING IN THE TAIL

The rising sun quickly climbs up the desert sky. As you lie in your tent, snug in your sleeping bag, you can see the canvas around you turning pale in the dawn light: the air of the desert night is chill on your face. Outside there is nothing to hear but the soft hiss of sand stirred by the rising breeze. It is wonderful to be here in North Africa, with the mighty Atlas mountains to the north, their peaks just over the horizon, and the sand sea of the Sahara flowing away from you towards the south.

Time to rise, brew the tea and bake some gritty Arab bread in the sand. Then you must load the Range Rover and set out for the wells at Sba. You reach for your boots lying by the doorflaps of the tent. As you pull on the left one, you feel what might be a crumpled ball of paper beneath your toes. Almost at once, before you can take off the boot to investigate, you feel the blaze of pain erupt. You have been stung! With a violent kick you send the boot flying from your foot. A clay-coloured object, crab-like, falls out of it and scuttles hesitantly away under the tent wall. The pain in your foot mounts rapidly. You begin to sweat . . .

You have just been injected with poison by a scorpion, one of the most deadly kind at that – the *fat-tailed scorpion*.

Nobody's friend

Scorpions are *not* popular. They are regarded with loathing and fear by most people, although I have seen folk in North Africa catch them, pluck off the venomous

Loaded with poison! The sting of a dangerous desert scorpion.

sting at the tip of their tails, and pop them in their mouths to eat with relish as you might scoff a boiled prawn.

Scorpions form a most ancient family of animals, the first spider-like creatures to leave the oceans to live on land. Unlike insects which have six legs, they have eight. About 650 different living species of scorpion are known to science, ranging from harmless ones, through painful ones, to ones that can be killers! They are found in all warm parts of the world, particularly deserts, and extend up into Europe as far north as southern Austria and Germany. There is even a (harmless) immigrant colony of small scorpions living in the gravel between the railway lines near a station in the south of England!

All scorpions are more or less alike in appearance. They have powerful pincers or pedipalps, that resemble the claws of a lobster but which can do you no harm. There are four to six pairs of eyes on the armoured head.

The scorpion's tail (actually part of the abdomen or tummy) is built of five segments with an expanded, curved tip that contains two big venom glands and is drawn out into a sharp sting perforated by two fine venom ducts. Large species of scorpion possess large stings and inject

lots of venom, but this isn't necessarily as powerful in its effects as the more concentrated venom of some smaller species. The venoms of most scorpions attack the nervous system, eventually causing paralysis of essential muscles, though some forms also affect the blood and circulation system.

When it is hungry, the scorpion seizes an insect such as a locust with its pincers, brings the tail sting over its head to stab the victim, mashes it with its mouthparts and injects digestive enzymes into the wound. The enzymes turn all the inside tissues of the insect into a liquid soup which is then pumped out and strained by the powerful gullet of the scorpion. Nothing but the husk-like shell of the insect remains. Scorpions feed on spiders, millipedes and other scorpions as well as insects, but can go hungry for more than a year without dying.

Although the scorpion mainly uses its sting to subdue its prey, it is also used to defend itself from other animals on the look out for a tinned meal! But it is not always effective: some animals are resistant to scorpion venom. These include the *European hedgehog* and the *gerbil* (300 times less sensitive to the poison than a guinea pig). *Dogs* are easily poisoned, but the *fennec fox* is immune.

The scorpion's main enemies include *ants* (mass attacks by ants rapidly overpower them), *toads, lizards, birds, foxes, bats, rodents* and *monkeys*. I have seen farmyard *chickens* in Arizona calmly dismembering scorpions with their beaks.

Deadliest scorpions

The biggest kinds of scorpion such as the *lobster scorpion* of the Sumatran jungle and the gleaming *black Pandinus* of Africa, another forest dweller, can attain lengths of 25-30 cm from tips of pincers to tip of sting, but rarely if ever cause human fatalities. Nor do the very smallest ones like *Microbuthus* of the Red Sea coast, which rarely exceeds 13 mm in length. The trouble comes from some of the medium-sized scorpion species.

There are more species of scorpion than spider that are dangerous to humans and in North America far more people are killed by scorpions than by snakes, although there are only two really dangerous species in that part of the world. In Arizona, over a 21-year period, about three people a year died from scorpion venom with most deaths in July when

The scorpion has lots of natural enemies such as this mongoose which can kill it quite easily.

people were more likely to be out and about in the wide open spaces where scorpions live.

Probably the most dangerous of all scorpions is the *fat-tailed scorpion* of North Africa. The venom can kill a man in about four hours and a dog in seven minutes. Nowadays, thanks to the existence of

The dramatic-looking but not very venomous
Pandinus *scorpion of Africa grabs a caterpillar.*

antidotes (anti-venins) to scorpion venom, only about 1 per cent of scorpion stings in North Africa prove fatal, though tens of thousands of people are stung every year. In Africa as in South America, most scorpion stings are inflicted upon the bare feet of people.

Fight to the death

Scorpions are loners, avoiding one another like the plague except for the brief mating period. Put two scorpions together in a small vivarium and they will inevitably fight to the death with the victor winning by brute force, not by injecting its venom, and then usually eating his vanquished opponent. The story that scorpions commit suicide by stinging themselves to death when surrounded by a ring of fire is untrue, but they are not completely immune to their own poison. A fat-tailed scorpion, however, requires 200 times more of its own venom to kill itself than it would have to inject into a guinea pig to kill it. The explanation for the 'ring of fire suicide' fable is that, trapped by flames, a scorpion first tries to escape and, failing this, then begins to strike frantically with its tail as if in an attempt to sting. Finally it becomes insensitive, overcome by the heat, and will die unless rescued and allow to recover.

Although largely unloved, the scorpion is a remarkable and successful creature with a long history behind it. You may never see one outside the invertebrate house at the zoo, but even if you do, the chances of your being stung, still less seriously injured by one, are very small indeed.

However, as scorpions, like spiders, have a habit of entering human habitations and secreting themselves under carpets, in shoes, etc., if you are visiting or live in a country where scorpions are common, it might just be worth shaking out your slippers before you put them on in the morning! They are nocturnal creatures who, in the open, live under logs or rocks and go hunting at night when fewer of their many enemies are about.

> *My father hath chastised you with whips, but I will chastise you with scorpions.*
>
> *Old Testament*
> Kings I, Chapter 12, Verse ii

28

The sea hides many master animal poisoners, some more deadly than the great white shark or the killer whale – and infinitely more subtle. Here however we must distinguish between creatures that are venomous – that deliver their venom to a victim or foe by sting, bite or some other device; and those that are merely poisonous – that can make people or other animals that eat them, ill, perhaps fatally so.

In recent years as a zoo vet travelling round the world, I have had to deal with several cases involving both venomous and poisonous marine creatures. First there was a dolphin in Indonesia that had been fed accidentally on a fish with the boring Latin name of *Arothron hispidus*. The fish poisoned the dolphin – you'll begin to see why when I tell you that the English name for that fish is *deadly death puffer*. Then in Cuba in 1987 I was asked to go and examine a human, a young man who, while wading across a shallow river estuary with bare feet, trod on a flat fish, with a long thin tail, that was lying on the bottom. It was a *stingray*. Characteristically, the fish whipped its tail upwards and forwards and jabbed the man's leg with a barbed poison needle injecting him with venom. When I saw the poor fellow he was in great pain with a red, inflamed leg, three times its normal size from toes to thigh.

Fugu food poisoning

There are many species of fish which are poisonous to eat, but the deadly death puffer is one of the most dangerous – and it claims many human victims every year, often through their own fault!

Scientists recognise about 90 different species of puffer fish. They are often plumpish, brightly coloured and strikingly marked animals, with mouths that remind me of a parakeet's, and some are covered with hedgehog-like prickles. They all possess one remarkable ability: they can inflate themselves – literally puff themselves up into a balloon shape –

One kind of fugu, the puffer fish.

Dangerous but delicious food: the preparation of fugu.

by gulping large quantities of water or air. While they are doing this they make considerable noise by grinding their teeth together! This puffing-up behaviour is a defence against predators that might be tempted to swallow them whole.

The puffer fish is one of the most poisonous of all marine mammals but the poisonous chemicals do not occur everywhere in its body. They are located principally in the skin, liver, sex organs and intestines. So how do people get poisoned? In Japan, puffer fish, called *fugu*, is greatly prized as a very tasty (and very expensive) dish, eaten raw. Special chefs in fugu restaurants, who have spent nine years being trained how to recognise and cut away the lethal parts of the fish, serve up plates of the grey-white flesh cut very thin and beautifully arranged in the shape of flying birds, flowers, trees, etc. Even so, faint traces of the poison remain: this is usually not enough to make a person ill, but is sufficient to produce a light numbing of the eater's lips (a bit like eating a very hot curry). Japanese gourmets relish the experience, *but* occasionally something goes wrong – an inexperienced chef is let loose on the customers or folk try to prepare the fugu themselves at home. Fugu is the main cause of food poisoning in Japan. Sixty per cent of people who are poisoned in this way will die. There is a famous two-line Japanese poem which makes the point simply:

Last night he and I ate fugu,
Today I help carry his coffin.

Puffer fish are most numerous in tropical seas, but many species do extend into temperate zones including the Mediterranean, the Atlantic coast of Portugal and United States waters. Puffer fish can be seen in good marine aquaria such as the ones at London Zoo, Marineland, Spain and Sea World, USA.

Venomous fish

Stingrays cause more human injuries each year than all the other kinds of fish put together. Most are found in salt water but one species regularly enters coastal rivers. They are flat, broad fish with a stinging tail that is used to defend themselves. They lie partly buried in muddy or sandy bottoms, feeding on shellfish and worms. Trouble occurs when you accidentally stand on or try to handle one of these creatures. The stinging organ of the ray is situated on the upper surface of the tail and consists of a spiky, barbed spine within a skin sheath. The underside of the spine is grooved and the grooves are lined with a spongy tissue that manufactures the venom. When the sting is brought into play, the spine flicks out of its sheath as the tail whips upwards and forwards, scorpion-like. The wound produced by the stinging spine can be as long as 18 or even 20 cm.

Although the stingray poison causes severe pain, nausea and weakness, and may affect the circulatory and nervous systems of the victim, death rarely ensues. Stingrays are found all around the USA, Central and South America, in African and Far Eastern oceans, the Mediterranean and in Europe as far north as Scandinavia.

The most venomous of all fish is the *stone-fish*. This is an ugly-looking bottom-dweller with a broad, flat head, sharply tapered body, blunt tail and a warty skin covered with slime. It is a master of disguise and lies camouflaged and immobile, usually against a rocky or coral background, virtually invisible to the eye. When its prey, an unsuspecting fish or prawn, comes along, the stone-fish lunges forward with incredible speed and snaps up the victim in its capacious mouth. So it uses its disguise not its venom to get its dinner. Again, like the stingray, the stone-fish uses its venom to protect itself from danger. It carries poison spines along its back and in its fins. Each spine

'Stand on me and I'll stab your leg!' A stingray off the coast of Minorca.

has two bags of venom near the tip. When the spines are erect, a slight touch to the tip will trigger the discharge of venom which flows along the grooves and into the victim's wound. As stone-fish live in shallow water, often in tidal pools and by reefs, in tropical seas, many cases of poisoning occur when bathers or paddlers accidentally brush past them or step on them. Stone-fish venom is extremely powerful and produces excruciating pain, collapse and often death. Luckily antivenins now exist which doctors can use effectively to treat an affected person.

There are many other kinds of venomous fish that deliver poison by means of spines including the *weever, scorpion fish, zebra fish, toad fish* and *wasp fish*. However, out of around 25,000 species of fish living in the oceans, fewer than a hundred are dangerous to man.

Ugly, well-disguised and lethal – the world's most dangerous fish, the stonefish, lurks on the sea bed.

Stinging tentacles

The sea is the home of other animal poisoners besides fish. One of the prettiest is the *cone shell*, a sea-snail that can launch a poisonous javelin if it feels molested. Then there are the *jelly fish*, including the spectacular and much feared *Portuguese man o'war*. This strange creature, actually not a true jelly fish but a colonial organism (one animal composed of many tiny animals), has a blue-bottle float and tentacles that can be several metres in length. The tentacles bear numerous stinging mechanisms which cause pain, cramps and other nervous symptoms if someone is unlucky enough to contact them with naked skin. Portuguese Men

O'War must taste nice to sea turtles however, for they love to gobble them down even though the stinging tentacles make their eyes sore and puffy for a time.

The most dangerous jelly fish is the *box jelly fish* or *sea wasp*. These inhabitants of Australian and Philippine waters and the Indian Ocean, have stinging tentacles that can kill extremely quickly, by means of a poison that attacks the nervous system. Other nasty stingers are the *sea nettle* and *sea blubber*. Although the sea blubber can sometimes be found in colder waters, the sea wasp and sea nettle prefer tropical seas. The tiny needles of the jelly fish stinging apparatus are unable to penetrate fine nylon, so a body stocking or tights give excellent protection to swimmers in places where dangerous 'jellies' are to be found.

A delicate yet violently venomous veil: the sea wasp drifts through the ocean.

INVISIBLE AND DEADLY

The family counted themselves doubly fortunate; the day they had chosen for their picnic had turned out to be the best so far that summer, with a cloudless sky, blue as a kingfisher. The sun's heat was tempered by a silken breeze, and the spot they had found on the lochside was perfect, carpeted with lush green grass bespeckled with tiny speedwell and buttercups, and fringed by low bushes, with not a soul in sight.

While father took the children down to the water's edge in search of frogs and sticklebacks, mother spread the rug and unpacked the hamper. Lunch promised the usual delights – Orkney cheese, pickled onions, slices of chicken, meat paste sandwiches and apples, washed down with lemonade or cider. The woman took the bread and butter slices out of a grease-proof bag and laid them on a serving plate. Then she began opening the tin of meat paste. 'Lovely,' she thought, 'real game paste full of chunky venison and wild duck and pheasant.' She had bought the paste at a bargain price the day before because the label was peeling and the tin rusting. 'It's what's inside that counts,' she had reckoned. 'You don't eat the label or the tin.'

The rich smell of the paste as she spread it evenly on the slices made her mouth water.

Half an hour later she called to the others. Lunch was ready. Before very long they all sat happily eating and drinking, drenched in the golden light of the midday sun. It was the daughter who first noticed something odd while she was helping her mother clean up after the meal. 'Mum, I think I'm going to be sick,' she said. The girl felt dizzy.

'I don't feel all that good either,' said the father, and he did look distinctly pale . . .

When the sun at last melted and drained away, blood crimson, behind the hills, the family were still by the lochside, lying on the grass. There was no sound

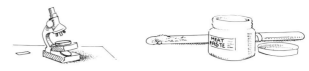

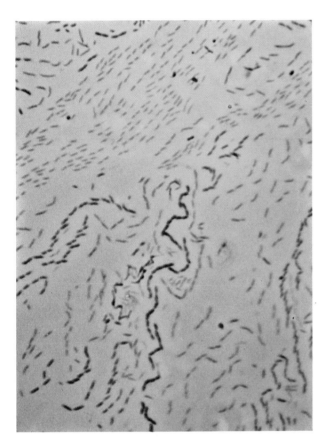

Under the microscope the C. botulinum *bacteria looks like spilled beads from a necklace.*

but the lapping of the water and the cry of a far-away curlew. No-one stirred. They could not. Their lives had ended in mid-afternoon, snuffed out by a powerful poison manufactured by a living creature that they could not possibly have seen.

What you have just read is a *true* story, but not a case of murder. There was, nevertheless, a culprit, a culprit so small as to be invisible without the aid of a powerful microscope. Its name was *C. botulinum*, a kind of bacterium or germ with a body only a few microns (a micron is one thousandth of a millimetre) in length.

Simplest form of life

What are bacteria? They are the commonest and simplest form of life on earth. They consist of minute single cells that are spherical, curly-wurly, oblong or cylindrical in shape. They are to be found everywhere – in air, water, soil, on and inside plants, animals and many non-living things. They are living creatures that scientists nowadays regard as being more closely related to plants than animals though they contain none of the green colouring matter (chlorophyll) found in all plants except fungi. Perhaps then bacteria can be regarded as a primitive fungi.

There are tens of thousands of different kinds of bacteria, most of them harmless to man and animals and many essential in maintaining the world as we know it. These latter enrich the soil, aid the growth of plants and help to break down waste matter. 'Good' bacteria enable man to make cheese and butter and increasingly to manufacture chemicals for industry and medicine. Some bacteria however, cause disease in man and animals. Blue whales and baboons, lions and locusts, beetles and bears – every animal on earth can suffer from bacterial illnesses.

Bacteria, like all living things, require food, and they feed by absorbing the necessary chemicals from the environment around them. To do this effectively they need moisture. They also prefer warmth, multiplying faster as the temperature rises. Few can grow or multiply below 5°C. They can survive however for a long time in ice or even when frozen down to –252°C. They hate being hotter than 38-48° C, dying usually (with a few exceptions) at temperatures of 50-65°C. Some bacteria need oxygen to thrive, others don't like it at all and do best in the absence of oxygen.

Bacteria multiply without mating. They simply split into two. Some split in this way every 20-30 minutes. Thus one single bacterium can become one billion bacteria after 15 hours! Such a mass of germs, called a colony, would occupy a space of about 1 cubic mm and could be seen with the naked eye. If multiplication continued, there would be enough to fill an egg-cup after a day and at the end of 35 hours the bacteria would occupy a space of 1,000 cubic metres – equivalent to the volume of a goods train with 100 wagons!

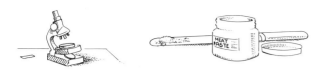

Two kinds of bacteria, rod-like bacilli *and bead-like* streptococci.

Why then don't we see the world swamped by bacteria? The answer is simple: firstly their multiplication depends on inexhaustible supplies of food, which is impossible; secondly bacteria produce chemical bi-products as they grow, many of which are acid, and ironically acids have the property of suppressing bacterial multiplication.

Botulism

Some disease-causing bacteria produce poisonous chemicals. In some bacteria, these poisons are either kept within their bodies (endo-toxins), and in others the poisons are sent out into the environment around them (exo-toxins). *C. botulinum*, our microscopic lochside poisoner, is an exo-toxin producing bacteria. Its poison is one of the most dangerous known to science and it remains effective even when the germs that made it are killed by, say, antibiotics. The illness caused by this bacterium is called botulism. Luckily it is uncommon in human beings, though it does affect animals from time to time.

The germ looks like a little rod or drumstick under the microscope. It can be found in the soil and the intestinal contents of herbivores (plant-eating animals) all over the world, and in these situations it doesn't cause any trouble. It is only when it comes into contact with decaying animal or plant matter that it will sometimes start to make its lethal poison as it feeds and multiplies. When an animal or person eats food contaminated with the poison, symptoms of illness quickly appear. This type of poisoning due to bacteria is *not* the same as an infection where the bacteria themselves have to enter the patient's body and multiply to cause the disease.

In the case of the tragic family picnic which I described earlier, the rusting tin of meat paste must have had a hole in it through which the botulism germs entered before starting to feed on the contents. This was a very rare occurrence. Tinned food is normally very safe to eat. It is sealed airtight and heat treated to sterilise completely the food inside. But if tins are damaged or if they become rusty when stored for too long a period, the airtight seal may sometimes be broken and the bacteria that abound in the outside world can then find their way in.

C. botulinum is one of a family of poison-manufacturing germs that cause sickness and death in man and animals. Nowadays animals which are at risk from these dangerous 'bugs' can be protected by vaccines which are injected.

DANGER ON EIGHT LEGS

The mouse had been out in the dry river bed by moonlight searching for seeds and all the while hoping that the owls were too busy elsewhere to come looking for him. Now, his appetite satisfied, he hurried towards his home under the rock, a safe haven that was dry and warm, lined with yellowing grass. Time for a nap. He slipped into his hole and moved down the familiar short corridor, its walls polished smooth by his fur. After barely 10 cm the corridor opened out into the apple-sized nesting chamber where he would curl up; his whiskers twitched furiously in anticipation.

STOP! His sensitive nose and ears and the twitching whiskers simultaneously rang alarm bells. Something, someone, was in his nest! Good grief – he knew what it was, though it was cloaked in blackness. A spider – a big, *bird-eating spider* – the sort that sometimes kills and feeds on baby mice, the sort that had a nasty habit of squatting in homes that properly belonged to mice!

Well, so be it. *He* was no baby mouse. *He* had been around, and he felt quite confident about taking on this spider, killing it with his sharp teeth, and maybe eating it tomorrow for his lunch. He sensed that the spider was already on guard and facing him. The front pair of its eight legs would be raised, the massive venom-injecting mouthparts ready. Okay, so he'd lunge towards the left, to take a nip at the spider's side. There, aha! His opening attack worked – his nose hit the spider and knocked it off balance. Now to snap for one of the raised legs, well out of reach of the sickle-shaped jaws. What was that . . . a soft scratching sound? He couldn't make sense of it – the spider seemed to be scratching its big round bottom. Why? The air of the chamber, normally fresh and fragrant, was suddenly filled with pain and fire. He breathed in and it was like inhaling a cloud of glass splinters. The mouse sneezed violently. The pain remained. Breathing was so difficult. His nose must surely be aflame. Sneezing repeatedly the mouse staggered back up the corridor.

The spider, for once, had won – and it hadn't had to use a single drop of the poison in its jaws.

Toothless bite

Spiders are carnivores, preying upon insects and other creatures. They don't have teeth and cannot swallow solid mat-

Somebody's squatting in my apartment!

37

The 'Tarantula' of horror movies fame, this bird-eating spider is not really dangerous to man.

ter. But most spiders are equipped with poison – not in a sting, but in their biting mouthparts. In fact there are only two families of spider that have no venom glands at all. When hungry, they seek for prey either by ambushing it, constructing a web to trap it, or actively hunting it. Then they kill the victim with a bite (spiders that make webs don't normally use their poison when doing this) and inject digestive chemicals (enzymes) into the wound that liquefy the internal tissues of their victim. Then they pump the victim dry, leaving nothing but an empty shell. Spiders never feed on dead animals

though they can be fooled into feasting on a piece of meat by attaching it to a thin thread and dragging or dangling it in front of the spider to induce the latter to grasp it.

The majority of spiders, and there are about 40,000 species alive today, are not dangerous to man. In fact they are useful animals to have about, acting as unpaid insect pest controllers. There are however some very poisonous kinds to be found in certain countries which we must treat

with great respect. The big, hairy *bird-eating spider* that evicted the mouse at the beginning of this chapter and which often stars in horror films (wrongly named a 'tarantula'), looks dramatic but isn't much of a threat to people. True, its jaws are large and its bite can be painful if provoked, but these solitary, rather retiring spiders don't go looking for trouble and the effect of their venom is about the same as that of a bee sting. If annoyed or threatened bird-eating spiders scratch their rear ends with their hind legs knocking off some of the fine hairs that cover their globular abdomen. These hairs look like barbed harpoons under the microscope. They float in the air and are breathed in by an attacker (such as my

A female black widow spider guards three of her egg cocoons, which will hatch out 50-150 young.

mouse) causing instant pain and inflammation in the nostrils. The hairs may also sharply irritate skin and eyes if they come into contact with them.

The most venomous spiders in the world are far smaller than the much misunderstood bird-eaters. Probably the most notorious is the *black widow*, round and shiny like a ripe blackcurrant and emblazoned underneath with a distinctive red, hour-glass-shaped mark. This spider, found in the United States, Central and South America, Hawaii and the West Indies, inflicts an agonising bite which can make a human being ill but is very rarely fatal. In the 218 years between 1726 and 1943 only 55 human deaths in the USA were reported to be caused by the black widow spider. If the anti-venins which are now available to doctors for use in cases of black widow

A surprising and deadly encounter: a red-back spider attacks and kills a small tree snake.

poisoning had been available then, most of those victims would have been saved.

Spiders more unpleasant than the black widow do exist. Top of my list of spider 'baddies' is the *brown recluse* or *fiddleback spider* of the United States and Australia. Its bite is no more painful than a bee sting but it produces other more alarming effects, such as fever, and severe destruction and often infection of tissue in the area surrounding the bite. Infrequent human deaths have been attributed to this spider. Some scientists believe that the most dangerous of all spiders is the *comb* or *wandering spider* found all over South America. It is very aggressive, bites repeatedly and produces much tissue damage with its venom. Other dangerous species are the *brown* or *grey widow* of the USA, the *funnel-web spider* of Australia, the *button spider* of South Africa, the *flax spider* of Argentina and the *jockey* or *red-back spider* of Arabia and Australasia. Like all other venomous spiders, these species can control the flow of the poison.

With 99 per cent of all spiders being harmless to man, unless you live in an appropriate part of the world and *know* that there are black widows or fiddlebacks in the garden shed, there is no need to be frightened of or try to kill any spiders you come across in your daily life. Observe them, inspect them more closely with a magnifying glass, marvel at the many intricate designs of web that some of them make and then let them go on their way.

> *Little Miss Muffet*
> *Sat on a tuffet,*
> *Eating her curds and whey;*
> *There came a big spider,*
> *Who sat down beside her*
> *And frightened Miss Muffet away.*
>
> Old Nursery Rhyme

NEEDLES AND PINS

Last week I was poisoned by an animal! Don't worry – I'm okay; cancel those calls to Sherlock Holmes and Hercule Poirot. Not time yet for RIP David Taylor. I didn't have to go to hospital or jab myself desperately, alone and far from civilisation, with Death Adder anti-venin.

It's highly unlikely that you will ever be bitten by a snake, shrew or gila monster, stung by a sea wasp or scorpion, or jabbed by a platypus' poison spur. But, like me, you may very well at some time in your life, be injected with the poison of another kind of animal, an experience that is briefly painful but very rarely serious or even needful of treatment by a doctor. I refer to insect stings, like the one I got from a quick-tempered wasp!

Perhaps you or a friend of yours have flicked a hand at a wasp that was pestering you, when, say, you were eating a plum in the garden in early autumn. Away it buzzes to return almost at once in

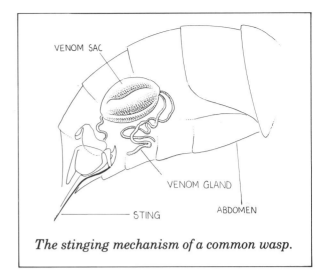

The stinging mechanism of a common wasp.

the hope of sharing the ripe fruit which it can smell through its antennae. And then – zap – for some reason, it lands on the flicking hand and delivers a short, sharp sting! As neat as a nurse with a hypodermic syringe, it injects a tiny quantity of venom through a fine retractable needle on the tip of its abdomen.

Single bee stings are rarely serious but here, drastic measures had to be taken against a dangerous swarm of killer bees.

Ouch! The honey bee stings and withdraws, leaving its 'needle' stuck in the skin.

Swarm attack

Insects that can sting in this way include the wasp, bee, hornet and ant. More people die each year from bee and wasp stings than are killed by snake bites. Single bee or wasp stings hurt but are not serious except in rare cases where the victim is sensitive to the insect's venom. When disturbed, these insects can attack en masse and will persistently chase after a frantically fleeing victim for several kilometres. Sometimes folk have been stung by swarms of hundreds of bees and the record is thought to be held by a man who survived an attack by over 2,200 bees; he saved himself by jumping into a river and staying submerged for four hours with only his nose above the water's surface.

A very aggressive bee is the so-called *killer bee* of South America. In the mid-1950s, *African bees*, aggressive creatures, were sent to Brazil in the hope of improving that country's honey production. Some of them escaped and bred with the local bees to produce a most vicious cross-bred bee that has the habit of attacking in very large numbers when it loses its cool. Unfortunately this occurs quite frequently. Swarms of the militant insects have since spread steadily northward towards the USA at a rate of about 300 km per year, interbreeding with native species in the regions through which they pass, to create ever greater numbers of killer bees. Between 200 and 300 persons in Brazil have been killed by these dangerous bees since their arrival. The bees attack continually, inflicting about 60 stings per minute for up to three hours. In one Brazilian town which was visited by an angry, buzzing horde, firemen in asbestos suits had to fight them with army flame-throwers!

Also in the South American jungle lives a *giant red bee* whose sting is said to be so powerful it can kill a jaguar. In India and Sri Lanka, the *large rock bee* is greatly feared. Rock bees, when annoyed, sting so badly that special protective cages are provided at the ancient fortress of Sigiriya in Sri Lanka, to which humans can retreat when the bees are up in arms. On the cages are signs saying – 'shelter in case of bee attack'.

Bees, like wasps and ants, use their stings for defensive purposes and possess especially large venom glands to supply their stinging needles. The venom con-

tains a chemical called formic acid. Some other insect venom comprises different chemicals including ones that act in ways similar to those of cobra venom.

In Sweden there is a very large wasp, the *Geting*, which delivers a most painful sting and in Africa some areas are inhabited by very easily upset hornets. It is virtually impossible to work in the vicinity of the nests of these insects without being attacked.

Marching ants

Ants are the most abundant social insect on earth with about one million billion alive at any given time. Some ants can not only bite painfully but also carry a significant sting. Certain ant species, the *army ants* of South America and the *driver ants* of Africa, periodically go on great marches in hordes that can number many millions. Such an ant army may be 8 km in length advancing on a 3 km-wide front, killing and eating any creature that they come across and which isn't quick enough to move out of their way. Tethered goats and horses have been devoured by these terrible invaders. The ants in these armies behave in a remarkably disciplined military fashion, performing 'manoeuvres' such as pincer-movements (splitting the advancing column into two wings) to outflank and surround an 'enemy' with 'professional soldiers' in the form of specialised warrior ants marching at the head and sides of the massed ranks.

A column of army ants marching across a field in Costa Rica.

The ferociously biting bulldog ant displays its long mouthparts.

Ants working together like this can often best be considered as one single 'animal' composed of interdependent parts like cells in a human body. An average driver ant colony numbers around 20 million individuals and tips the scales at about 20 kg.

Some of the most unpleasant of all ants are the *black bulldog ants* of Australia which generally bite and sting at the same time, and the *fire ants* of South America and the southern USA. Fire ants sting tenaciously, leaving their 'needles' in the victim's flesh for up to 25 seconds while they pump in their venom. The venom has the property of deterring the white blood cells that are an important part of the body's defence against infections, and so fire ant stings will often result in a nasty skin disease. More than 65 million hectares of the southern USA are infested with this insect, and in parts there are 400 fire ant hills per hectare.

Other venomous insects

There are many other venomous sorts of insect. One highly sinister creature, a desert bug given the Hebrew name *Afrur*, is said to be perhaps the most venomous animal on earth. The bug has venom glands that occupy most of its body and which manufacture a chemical hundreds of times more lethal than cobra venom!

Some insects are poisonous only in the immature or larval stages of their life. The grub of *diamphidia*, a beetle found in the Kalahari Desert of Africa, contains a powerful poison which is extracted from them and rubbed onto the tips of the hunting arrows of the bush men who live in those parts. Several moths, including the *puss moth* of the southern United States, have caterpillars covered with 'fur'. Some of these hairs are linked to venom glands in the skin. Contact with such caterpillars can produce rashes, pain and feverish illness in humans or domestic pets, particularly in sensitive individuals. Other moth caterpillars with irritant poisons are to be found in Africa, Asia and Europe.

ARROWS AND DARTS

The Indian stood utterly motionless beneath the tree. Far above the dark green gloom paled, in small patches where the daylight struggled to penetrate the innumerable layers of leaves and cascades of grey vines. Presently he saw what he was looking for. A woolly monkey sat on the black branch as if in deep thought. The Indian watched it and slowly raised the 2 m long cane pipe to his lips. It pointed up towards the monkey like a giant's pale finger. The man inhaled deeply and then puffed out his cheeks. There was a soft hiss as he blew.

High above, the woolly monkey sprang from the branch and effortlessly caught hold of a vine. Its momentum caused the vine to swing and the monkey went with it. It was almost within arms' length of another branch, reaching out to take hold, when it abruptly seemed to lose all energy. It missed the branch and its legs flailed uselessly. With a loud crashing of twigs and the whoosh of disturbed leaves, the monkey hurtled to the ground where it lay motionless. 'Good,' thought the Indian, 'at last some meat for my people.' He picked up the dead monkey and slung it over one shoulder. He and his wives and his children would soon sit eating by the fire in the clearing deep within the Amazon jungle. And the meal that they would enjoy would be thanks to a tiny, pretty and incredibly poisonous frog.

Ancient amphibians

Frogs and toads, my most *favourite* animals, are amphibians. Amphibians have descended from the animals which made the first epic move from life in the ocean to life on land. They were the first vertebrates (animals with backbones) to adapt partially to a terrestrial lifestyle. Modern amphibians such as frogs and newts still have, you might say, one foot on land and the other in water. They are cold-blooded, air-breathing animals with naked, moist, unscaled skins through which they can absorb oxygen. Their skin is rich in slime-producing glands, which help to keep them moist when out of the water. Most amphibians have four legs. Their eggs, which do not have shells like those of reptiles, are laid in water (or moist places) and hatch into larvae which pass through an aquatic existence before metamor-

I've got so much news to tell you! Close encounters of the marine toad kind.

phosing (changing their bodies) into the adult form.

Frogs and toads range in size from certain species of South American *arrow frogs* which are only 8-12 mm long, to the *Goliath frog* of West Africa which can attain a length of 35 cm and a weight of over 3 kg. The familiar *marine toad*, now widely distributed in many parts of the world and the *Blomberg toad* of Colombia, both of which will eat rats and can give humans who mishandle them painful bites may weigh up to 1.25 kg. In South America large marine toads come out at night in some towns to sit under street lights to catch moths and other insects attracted by the glow. Each toad has its own street light which it defends.

Toxic slime

Although never equipped with a venomous bite, some frogs and toads, though a tiny minority of the total number of species, are extremely poisonous. Most amphibians secrete some poison in their skin, but a few have developed this, for defensive reasons, to an extreme degree. The animal is kept moist when out of water by mucus-producing glands lying within the skin; the poison is contained within this mucus or slime. *Poison-arrow frogs*, the most poisonous frogs of all, make highly toxic slime all over the body while toads such as the marine and *Colorado River* species concentrate it in glands behind the eye. The poisonous secretions

I know I'm the handsomest creature on earth! A male poison arrow frog puffs out his throat as he calls.

discourage other animals from eating them; a dog eating a marine toad might well be killed by the poison which affects the action of the heart. The Blomberg toad can actually spray the poison liquid out of its head glands, and a person or animal hit in the eye would suffer at least painful irritation and at worst be made temporarily ill. The pretty, spotted *North American Pickerel frog* has a sticky skin which is covered with a fluid that is deadly to other frog species and harmful to most small animals.

Here is a list of some of the really dangerous frogs:

1 The strawberry poison-arrow frog.
2 The yellow-spotted frog.
3 The golden poison-arrow frog.
4 Zatek's frog.
5 The three-striped poison-arrow frog.

Snug as bugs in our toadstool head! Two poison arrow frogs take it easy.

But the worst of all is the Two-toned poison-arrow frog or *Kokoa* of the dense jungles of Colombia. It has the doubtful honour of producing perhaps the most active of all animal poisons. One ten thousandth of a gram of its poison would kill a man. You remember how the Amazonian Indian at the beginning of this chapter used a blow-pipe to fire a poison dart at a woolly monkey. The poison that tipped his dart came from a poison-arrow frog's skin.

In Colombia, Indians catch the tiny (only 20-30 mm long) Kokoa frog by imitating the high-pitched peeping noise it makes through whistling and tapping their cheeks at the same time. Fooled into thinking that there is a rival nearby, the Kokoa returns the call and can then be pinpointed and caught. The frogs are killed and roasted slowly over a fire until drops of poison ooze out of the skin. The tips of hunting arrows and darts are dipped into this liquid, which is then left to dry on. One frog produces enough poison for about 50 darts. With their arrows and darts the South American Indians go hunting for jaguar, deer and birds as well as monkeys.

Although the poison-arrow frog poison is not normally effective when applied to unbroken skin or swallowed by mouth, there are some species which are apparently dangerous to handle. I myself have seen a colleague develop mild symptoms of poisoning after holding a red poison-arrow frog in the palm of his hands for a few minutes. Perhaps he had minute cuts or abrasions in his skin through which the poison entered his bloodstream, but it

may be that *some* poison-arrow skin slime can penetrate unbroken skin.

Don't forget that all the frogs and toads you are ever likely to come across outside the zoological gardens, are harmless, useful and charming creatures that we should be glad to have around.

Toadstones

Toads were once associated with poison in another way. Small stones that resembled a toad in colour or shape were believed in olden days to have come from the heads of very old toads. These 'toadstones' were worn as jewels, often set in rings, and were thought to sweat and change colour if brought near anything containing poison. As well as supposedly protecting the wearer against poison, the stones were thought to make ill people better, particularly if they were suffering from the effects of animal bites and stings. In an ancient English manuscript the following is written: 'A toadstone, called crepaudia, touching any part envenomed by the bite of a rat, wasp, spider, or other venomous beast, ceases the pain and swelling thereof.'

Like a living jewel, a turquoise poison arrow frog sits on a leaf in the rain forest.

> *Sweet are the uses of adversity,*
> *Which, like the toad, ugly and venomous,*
> *Wears yet a precious jewel in his head.*
>
> Shakespeare *As You Like It* (Act II, Sc. i).

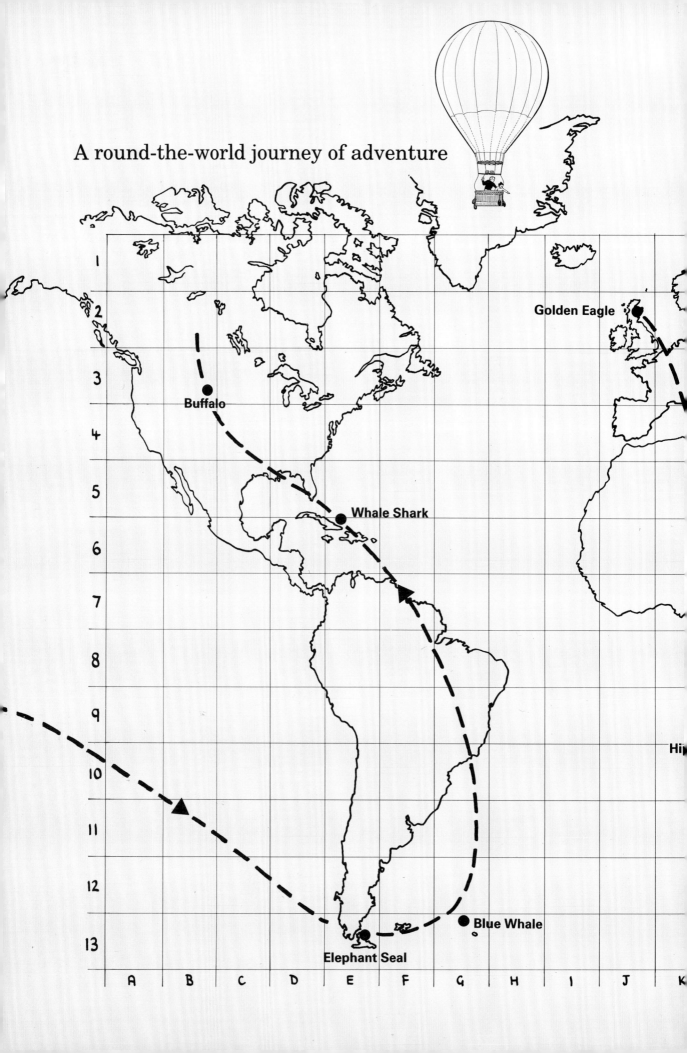

A round-the-world journey of adventure

Golden Eagle

Buffalo

Whale Shark

Hi

Blue Whale

Elephant Seal

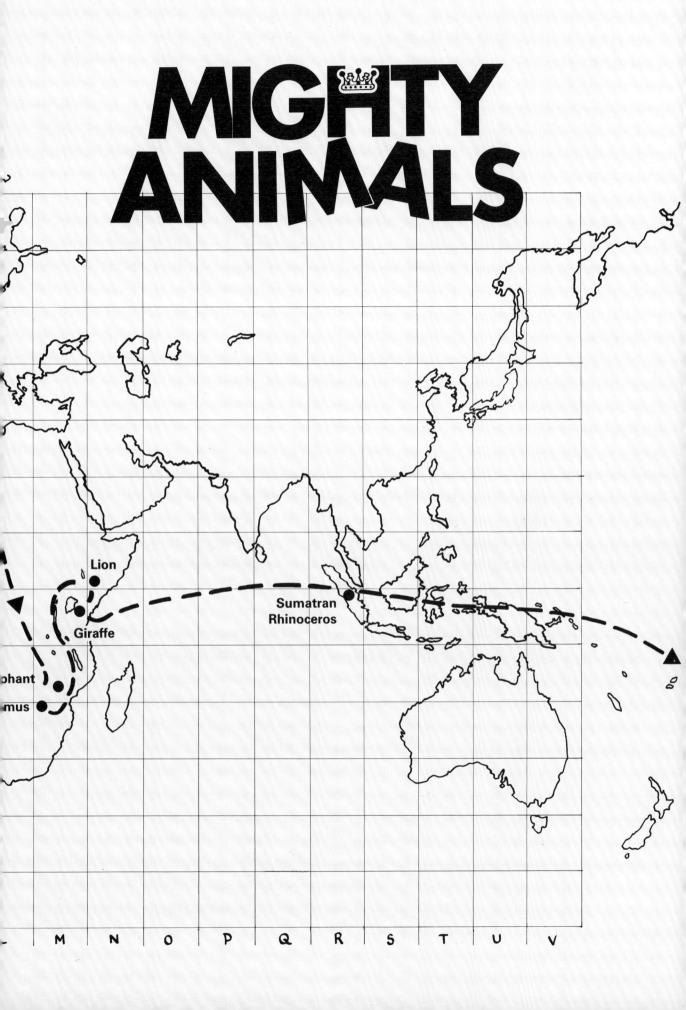

MIGHTY ANIMALS

*B*elow, gleaming gently in the early morning sun, the twin conical towers of a castle. We wave to a red-haired man who stands on the turreted ramparts gazing up at us as we drift by. The castle is perched on the edge of a broad expanse of gleaming black water beyond which gentle purple-tinged slopes press close to a range of mountains still smeared with snow. Although the mountainsides are, for the most part, heather-clad shoulders with fields of dark scree and eruptions of granite boulders, there is one place, a kilometre or so wide, where, aeons ago, the mountainside broke away to leave the high sheer cliffs of grey stone that our balloon is now approaching.

'Where are we, David?' you ask. I trim the burners and then look back at the castle.

'The fiery headed gentleman is, I believe, the owner of all the land we can see, but he *doesn't* own the magnificent

Emblem of a Roman legion – the proud eagle.

creatures we have travelled here to see.'

The balloon is now hanging almost motionless a few metres from the cliff face. It's tricky to hold it here. Pointing towards a rocky ledge where a jumble of dead twigs is lying, I'm about to explain when a shadow darkens the sky above us. There is a rush of wind, a short screech and two yellow claws snatch at my hair. Both of us tumble down in the basket as powerful dark wings beat overhead. The balloon starts to descend, yawing drunkenly. The shadow vanishes, the wind catches us and with relief I see the cliff's face begin to recede.

Above us, the sharp and gleaming eyes of the *golden eagle*, standing on the ledge with its chick in the eyrie (nest) beside it, glare at us and our curious craft.

The sun-bird

We are in the mountains of the north of Scotland. All of Britain's remaining and endangered golden eagles, with the exception of one pair that are now nesting in the Lake District of England, live in the Scottish hill country. Like some other birds of prey, they have suffered from persecution by egg collectors, the poisons and guns of gamekeepers and farmers, the increased use of pesticides in agriculture and the relentless spread of 'civilisation' into the once peaceful, wilder corners of the land.

From the earliest times, the eagle was venerated, feared and admired in almost every country where it existed. It was honoured in the ancient myths of Egypt, Persia, Assyria and India, and considered to be the associate of the great god Zeus of the Greeks. The Roman legions carried standards bearing the emblem of the eagle and when a Roman emperor died an eagle was let fly from his funeral pyre. Later the eagle took its place in the coat of arms of the Emperor Constantine, Queen Mary of England, of the states of Austria, Russia, Poland ('the Land of the White Eagle'), France and the United States – truly a noble bird. It was considered king of the heavens, the bringer of storms and

The golden eagle does not take kindly to visitors to its nest.

thunderbolts, the sun-bird who could stare into the sun's light without being dazzled. Many believed it never grew old because it was able, periodically, to renew its youth. It would first fly so near the sun that its feathers burst into flames, and then dive into the sea to quench the fire. Returning to its nest, it would patiently wait for the new plumage to grow, and with it, new youth.

The golden eagle is one of the best-known eagles and outside Scotland is also to be found in mountainous regions of continental Europe, Asia and North America. A pair of eagles build a huge nest (eyrie) of sticks on cliffs or tall trees, returning year after year to lay a clutch of 1-4 white eggs mottled with brown. The young are covered in white down which is replaced by dark brown juvenile plumage at about ten weeks of age. They moult annually until the wonderful golden brown colour of the adult is acquired at four years of age. The Tatar people of what is now Soviet Asia still hunt deer and wolves using golden eagles, and in Europe, in the days of medieval falconry, they were flown only by kings.

Lords of the air

Eagles, who hunt prey by day, are widely distributed around the world. There are

The golden eagle is the noblest of all hunting birds.

30 species of *booted* (with legs feathered to the toes) *eagle* in a family that includes the golden eagle, 11 species of *fish eagle*, including the endangered *white-tailed sea eagle* (now being reintroduced into the north of Scotland) and the famous *bald eagle* of the USA, 12 species of *snake-eating eagle* including the *bateleur* (juggler) *eagle* so named because of its aerial acrobatic skills during courtship, and several others such as the mighty *harpy eagle* of South America and the very rare, strange-faced, *monkey-eating eagle* of the Philippines, of which perhaps only a dozen or two still survive.

Although the golden eagle is an impressively big bird, with the heavier female weighing 6-7 kg and sporting a wingspan of up to 2.5 m, it isn't as heavy as the harpy eagle which sometimes reaches over 9 kg. Harpy eagles, however, need to hunt among trees, and so they have shorter (2.25 m), broader wings. The biggest wingspan among eagles is displayed by the *wedge-tailed eagle*, with some females claimed to have measured 3 m from tip to tip.

Could such great birds carry off human babies, as is so often alleged in old legends and fables? Experts think not. An 8 lb (3.63 kg) baby is probably too much for any living species of eagle, but ... *Steller's sea eagle* can lift seal pups, young Arctic foxes and large fish from sea or ground, harpy eagles can snatch up mammals such as monkeys, coati-mundis and opossums, a golden eagle has been seen to fly up with an adult fox (probably weighing something between 5 and 6 kg) in its talons, and American bald eagles are known to have carried off lambs and deer fawns.

The famous American bald eagle takes a meal of fish.

Eagles may not be stealers of infants, but they are expert at many other things. They can fly far and high; *steppe eagles* have been found at a height of 7,925 m on Mount Everest. Like all birds of prey, they have incredibly acute vision that is about three times sharper than yours and mine. Golden eagles are said to be able to spot a rabbit at a distance of 3 km and other species can pick out a grasshopper sitting motionless almost 300 m away. Like other birds, they can see in colour, but they cannot smell. (Some birds, such as the New World vultures, kiwis and petrels, are able to smell things.)

★ ★ ★ ★ ★

'Why do people deliberately kill eagles?' you ask as we move away.

'Well, often it's because of sheep farming. Eagles will feed on dead sheep that they come across, and sometimes take live

An American golden eagle feeds on a jack rabbit.

lambs. They rarely do much damage to flocks, but sheep farmers don't like losing even a single lamb. Eagles are nowadays protected in most countries, but illegal killing still goes on. And many die of pesticide poisoning. Like other birds of prey, they eat animals which carry the poisons in their bodies after eating seeds, fruits and vegetables sprayed with chemicals used in agriculture to control pests. These poisons build up in the eagles' bodies. Some, like DDT, make the shells of eggs laid by the birds too thin – so they break and kill the developing chick. Other pesticides, the more modern ones, attack various organs of the bird's body, producing illness and then death.'

'Same old story,' I hear you mutter. 'Why can't we leave animals alone?'

The eagle watches intently from afar as we begin to soar up into his realm.

Crack! crack! crack! The sound of fire crackers far below breaks the quiet of the sun-drenched morning. The basket rocks slightly and a splinter of wood comes spinning up to land in your hair.

Crack! We both go to the sides and peer over. Three hundred metres below, the savannah plain, paling to yellow in the late summer heat and dotted with untidy clumps of grey-green scrub, runs in all directions to the horizon.

There is another, even louder crack. Then I catch sight of them, three figures standing beside a grey-black mound. They are looking up and one is pointing a stick . . . not a stick! And the mound . . . I recognise the outline.

A modern tragedy – poachers steal an elephant's rightful property.

'Get down!' I yell and yank at the controls. The burners open their throats and the blue flames roar upward. We must gain height quickly. 'Get on the radio and call up the police on channel 9,' I throw the hand-microphone across to you. 'Tell them we've run into some poachers who don't like us interfering with their dirty business, and give them a map reference.'

Crack! This time I actually hear the bullet hum as it travels past the basket. But we are already rising rapidly.

Half an hour later, after making sure through our binoculars that the coast is now clear, the poachers having fled with their booty, we land and walk over to the grey mound we had seen from the sky. It is indeed the sad remains of one of our mighty animals. Bloody, jagged-edged craters yawn where the tusks have been hacked out of its head. Another *elephant*

has been brutally struck off the list of Africa's fast-shrinking herds.

Giants of yesterday and today

The elephant must surely be the mightiest land animal alive. Measuring up to 4 m high at the shoulder and weighing as much as 6½ tonnes, Jumbo is a magnificent creature. Long ago there were over 350 kinds of elephant in the world. Perhaps the most famous of these extinct forms was the *mammoth*. It was about as big as a modern *Indian* elephant with a high, pointed skull and unique, spiralling tusks whose tips pointed towards one another. The tusks were 3 to 4 m long and would each weigh over 100 kg, longer and heavier than those of the biggest living *African* elephant, but not as huge as the 5 m tusks that were carried by another long-gone elephant, the *Straight-tusked elephant* which inhabited northern Germany about two million years ago.

Mammoths lived in the Pleistocene epoch, 50,000 to one million years ago. They were adapted to a cold, Arctic climate, being covered with long yellow-brown, woolly hair that almost reached the ground, and with patches of thicker black hairs on the cheeks, flanks and abdomen. They had small furry ears and a short tail tipped with a tuft of long stiff bristles. During periods of warm weather, they migrated north to follow the ice fields, grazing on grasses, sedges, and other plants such as wild thyme, Alpine poppy and crowfoot.

There are two reasons why we know so much about the mammoths. Firstly, early man, who hunted them, left marvellous cave paintings of them. Secondly, and more dramatically, scientists have found the deep-frozen bodies of mammoths in the permanently icy soil of the Siberian tundra. Many are so well preserved that they look as if they died only yesterday, with fresh plant food still green and succulent in their stomachs. Most exciting of all is the possibility that one day in the future mammoths may live again! Scientists who specialise in genetic engineer-

ing are capable of extracting genetic chemicals, which still carry the hereditary 'blueprint' of complete mammoths, from preserved mammoth body cells, and could use these when fertilising an ordinary female elephant by artificial means. Imagine – 21-23 months later (the elephant pregnancy period is the longest of any mammal) – the modern world's first mammoth baby could be born – 1,000 centuries after its parents grazed the Siberian land!

The woolly mammoth – could it be re-created in the future?

Other extinct elephants include the *Mastodon*, an inhabitant of all continents except Australia. Many fossil *Mastodons* have been dug up in the USA and Canada. These animals, longer and lower than modern elephants, fed on leaves in the wet, lush ice-age forests. There was also the mini-elephant, a dwarf form found in the Mediterranean regions, the smallest being a 1 m high variety from Crete, and the biggest elephant so far discovered (in Kent), a giant that stood almost 5 m high. (A mini-elephant would have made a good pet!)

Replaceable teeth

As we turn away from the body of the poachers' victim, we notice that a small group of elephants has emerged from a

The leader of an elephant family is usually an old female.

stand of acacia trees some 500 m away. A big female, leader of the herd, is looking in our direction, her ears flapped forwards to act as receiving dishes to collect more sound and her sensitive trunk held up, S-shaped, to sniff the air for information about us. (Elephants are very short-sighted.) We can tell immediately, because of the big ears, that these are African elephants; the ears of Asiatic or Indian elephants are much smaller.

Elephants are members of a group of mammals called Proboscidea (animals with a proboscis – a long snout). Surprisingly, their closest *living* relative is the *hyrax*, a small furry animal, rather like a large guinea-pig, which lives in Africa and parts of Arabia.

Although elephants are vegetarians, they are not ruminants which chew the cud, and don't possess four stomachs like cows, buffalo or antelopes. They have a simple single stomach and digest their food mainly in the large intestine, rather like horses. To grind the tough branches, leaves and fibrous plants which they eat, they have enormous teeth, each one about as big as a house brick and weighing 2 to 5 kg. Only four teeth are in use at any one time. As the two teeth at the front wear down, they fall out and are replaced by two new ones moving forwards from the back of the mouth. Throughout its life an elephant can call on a total of 24 teeth; after they are all used up, an elephant in the wild will starve to death. Nevertheless elephants, both in the wild and in zoos, can reach an age of 70 years and perhaps more.

On the rampage

Elephants are intelligent animals and also have a good memory. Elephant friends that I only see once every year or two instantly recognise me and make a fuss, tickling me with their trunk tips, purring like enormous cats and even squeaking with delight.

Even so, they can be dangerous too, as lions, tigers – and humans, know to their cost. Male elephants are particularly tricky when they are in the curious state called 'musth'. This is a physiological phe-

nomenon, not well understood, that occurs usually once a year and can last for a few days or a few months. The bulls become restless and aggressive and secrete an oily liquid from glands on their temples. And of course elephants never like being harassed, threatened or teased.

The African elephant has big ears which it flaps forward when it charges.

Once in a while elephants get roaring drunk after eating overripe fruit, particularly that of the so-called Miracle tree. When they detect the rather boozy smell of the berries on the wind, they'll travel miles to hold a rather alcoholic feast. And I've had to treat tipsy elephants who stole overripe medlar fruit when I was travelling with them across Spain. Not an easy job. In 1974 a herd of about 150 drunken elephants who had imbibed illegal alcoholic liquor made by villagers in West Bengal went on the rampage, killing five persons and injuring a dozen more. All in all between 200 and 500 people are killed each year by wild elephants, the majority of them in Africa, and occasionally elephants in zoos attack their keepers.

A shrinking population

It is a sad fact that elephants themselves are under threat nowadays. Poachers still kill them, just to take their tusks which are then sold for fashioning into ivory ornaments and trinkets. Poaching alone has reduced the African elephant population by more than HALF during the 1980's, from 1.2 million to less than 600,000. About 100,000 African elephants are slaughtered by poachers every year!

Then there's the ever-diminishing elephant habitat. Men, with their agriculture and their development of land, have so reduced the space needed by elephants that they no longer find a welcome in their old haunts. With fewer trees to crop, less space to roam, elephants do more damage to the available vegetation. The result is that in some places they must survive with very little tree cover, and the unshaded African sun on their backs produces changes in their blood vessels that can lead to an early death.

This baby Indian elephant is only one day old.

RIVERBED BALLET DANCER

You are grumbling again. Despite what I consider to have been a perfect landing right on target, it is obvious you don't like *mud*.

'Of all places!' you repeat. 'A mud bank slap in the middle of a river.' Brushing off another cluster of flies, I walk round the basket and begin to pull in the shroud that is our deflated balloon.

'But I'm *exactly* where I plan to be,' I say. 'This is *it*! What's a little mud between friends?' Wordless, you shake a leg, caked in sticky brown mud, towards me.

'Ah. But think of the animals I have brought you to see.'

You look around at the broad, black river, the banks covered in tall grass, dark green bushes beyond. A white stork stands contemplating the water at the river's edge with total concentration. A pair of black vultures lazily ride a thermal above our heads. The evening sky is a vast canvas of some modern painter slashed with broad strokes of flamingo-pink, orange and pearl.

'Crocodile!' you cry. 'Sacred in ancient times – killer of horses and men – a mighty river animal. That's it!'

'Wrong!'

'What then? Surely this river is in Africa – or have we landed in the Americas, in which case it must be an alligator?'

'Africa yes. Alligators no. As I said, we've landed exactly where I planned – right on top of a mud bank which is the nursery for the young of one of Africa's most impressive animals – and, moreover, an underwater ballet dancer.' No wonder you look puzzled.

'Come on, put on your wetsuit – we'll take a dip in the river and see if I can introduce you to it.'

Still puzzled, you change into your scuba gear and I do likewise. Fortunately the water is clear and warm and the river bottom is only 5 m down. No crocodiles around, but plenty of freshwater turtles sculling about just above the mud and big shoals of tilapia fish. We crouch on the river bottom back to back, keeping our eyes peeled. Five minutes pass and then – is it? – yes, it is – materialising out of the distant gloom, floats, dances almost, a mighty form. You turn to watch as I nudge you. The creature ignores us as it passes, followed by another and then another. An underwater procession of

The 'mini' hippo – the pigmy hippopotamus.

Lumbering on land, the hippo prances elegantly underwater.

giants. Over 3 m long and weighing up to 3 tonnes or more, the hippos move through the water with the greatest of ease.

Glorious mud

The *hippopotamus* is the largest *even*-toed mammal alive on earth (pigs, camels, deer, giraffes, sheep and cattle also have an even number of toes on their feet, while horses, tapirs and rhinoceroses have an odd number). Its closest relative is the pig. There are two living kinds of hippo – the hippopotamus that inhabits African grasslands, rivers and lakes, and the *pigmy hippo*, a forest dweller found only in a few parts of West Africa. Long ago hippos similar to these modern species lived all over Europe and in some regions of Asia.

The smooth skin of the hippo is thick, but evaporates water up to five times quicker than that of humans. So, during the day, the hippo messes about in water to avoid losing serious quantities of body liquid, and goes to feed on land during the cool of the night.

Hippos feed on grass and other plants for about five to six hours during the night. They leave the water and trundle down 'hippo pathways' that they have made (and marked with piles of dung so they can smell their way if necessary in the darkness) which lead to 'hippo lawns' where they graze. These lawns may be up to 2 km inland or even farther, if there are mud wallows along the way which can be used to refreshen and moisten the skin. 'Mud, mud, glorious mud!' is truly their theme song.

A dentist's nightmare – a hippo saying 'Aarh!!'

During the day, therefore, the hippo lazes and dozes in the river. It can stay under water for around five minutes. Its eyes, ears and nostrils are placed on the top of its head, so that it can lounge in the water with just those organs protruding above the surface. Its bulky body in water has a specific gravity of approximately 1 (the same as fresh water), so it can move about easily without any risk of sinking like a rock or bobbing up like a cork. Hippos are surprisingly agile creatures who can swim quite fast. And under water they spring like ballet dancers!

When the hippos have passed us by I tap you on the shoulder and indicate that we should surface. We paddle to the bank where we sit and watch a dozen or so hippos who have hauled out on to the mud. A few birds, oxpeckers and egrets have landed on the backs of the hippos, who are totally unconcerned at being used as convenient platforms for feeding.

Nursery tales

Although they look placid, hippos can be very dangerous. It is particularly risky for people to approach the mud bank or sandbar nurseries or 'creches' on which young hippos and their mothers are lying. Getting too near solitary old bulls can also bring about a sudden, devastating charge. One snap of those immense jaws can cut a boat, or a man, in two.

Hippo society, like that of elephants, is organised on herd lines led by females. The female hippos command their territory from the central creche. Important breeding males live on surrounding nearby mud banks while young males take up properties farther away. Baby hippos are born either on land or in shallow water, and some births actually occur underwater. As soon as it's born, the baby paddles up to the surface to take its first breath.

Hippo mothers take great care of their babies who suckle their milk either on land or in the water, and often the babies

lie on their mother's back when they are in deeper water. Sadly, nearly half of all baby hippos die within the first year of life. But if they survive, they can live for over 30 years, and individuals of 40 or more have been recorded in zoos.

The claim that hippos sweat blood is without foundation, although they *look* sometimes as if blood is oozing out of their skins while they bask in the sunshine.

Get out of the way – fast! Charging hippos can be very dangerous.

However, the red liquid is not blood but rather a coloured sweat-like liquid which is, would you believe, a natural sun-tan oil! It is possible that it also has antiseptic qualities, because hippo wounds – they often get them when squabbling – heal quickly and cleanly even in the dirtiest water.

★ ★ ★ ★

It is time to return to the balloon to be off on the evening breeze.

EMBLEM OF POWER

*L*ate afternoon, and we are floating slowly through the warm air. Below is an expanse of green and gold savannah, broken here and there with outcrops of rock and clusters of grey-green trees. In the distance, smoke-grey, a line of hills shimmers in the haze. We are in Kenya now.

On we drift until, almost directly under our basket, you spot a small herd of zebra grazing in a tight knot and unaware of our presence, for our shadow is still far to the side of them. Then, as you scan the ground with your binoculars, you make a soft hissing noise.

'Quick, David,' you whisper. 'Look. Over there. *Lion*!'

About 150 m downwind from the zebras, a fine lioness is lying crouched behind the ruins of a broken termite mound. She is staring intently in the direction of the zebras. To her right, another lioness is concealed behind rocks. She also is watching the grazing equines.

'The King of Beasts,' I whisper back. 'We're in luck. That pair of females, act-ing in concert as they usually do, are about to launch an attack. Watch! We'll see the classic moves of a hunting cat – more or less the same as those of your pet cat at home when he's stalking a bird.'

Lionesses do most of the hunting that supplies the pride with food, and we settle to watch their standard hunting techni-que. First, having spotted the target, they approach cautiously, taking advantage of any available cover. That's where the ter-mite mound and rocks come in. This is followed by the so-called 'slink run'. Both lionesses leave cover and move swiftly nearer to the zebras, keeping their bodies flattened close to the ground. Each lioness reaches another 'ambush point' – in both cases a low bush. They pause again, for they are now within 30 m of the zebra who, though nervous, are still unaware of their presence. Now the big cats prepare themselves for the final stage. We can see the hind feet making treading move-

The powerful kick of a zebra can often cope with an attacking lion.

64

'I won't tell you again!' A lioness scolds her cub.

ments as if rehearsing the dash, the tail tips are twitching furiously and the eyes are fixed on the nearest zebra. Suddenly, the attack is launched. One lioness charges out of cover, keeping her body flat to the ground. The other female follows suit. They sprint across the open ground. Both are homing in on the same young zebra. The zebra herd wheels in a cloud of dust. Hoofs fly. The first lioness springs forward, keeping her hind feet on the ground for stability. She aims for a neck bite but . . . wham! The hind hoofs of a zebra stallion catch her in the chest. She's knocked off balance. The second lioness is momentarily confused. The zebras are now in full flight. The attack has failed.

Lions can reach speeds of 55 kmh, but only over short distances – no chance of catching the zebras this time. Because the prey can often outsprint them, only about one in three of such combined hunting forays by lions are successful. This means that the lion cubs will have to wait for their dinner, which can sometimes be serious. Many cubs starve to death during their first year of life.

Lordly but lazy

The lion has been traditionally respected and admired. The Messiah is referred to in the Bible as the lion of the tribe of Judah. In Islam, Ali, the prophet Mohammed's son-in-law was called the Lion of God for his religious zeal and great courage, an attribute shared with King Richard I of England, Richard Lion-heart. The lion was an emblem, too, of the resurrection stemming from an ancient belief that lion cubs are born dead and remain so for three days, after which the father breathes on them and they come alive.

In heraldry, the lion has always been the symbol of sovereignty and power. There are three lions in the arms of England and one red one in those of Scotland.

65

The lion is one of the commonest heraldic animals.

A crowned lion was King Henry VIII's badge, and a winged lion is the emblem of the City of Venice. Some fountains traditionally have their water issuing from the mouth of a lion. This is a very old custom dating back to the ancient Egyptians who thus symbolised the annual flooding of the Nile which happens when the sun is in the zodiacal 'house' of Leo, the lion.

Lions long ago were one of the most widespread mammals in the world, to be found right across the northern hemisphere. Until about 2,000 years ago they inhabited south-eastern Europe. In the twentieth century they have become extinct in the Near and Middle East, most of Asia and West Africa and in North and South Africa. *Atlas lions*, from the North African mountains, can nowadays only be seen in zoos such as those at Madrid, Spain and Port Lympne, England. There are five subspecies of lion living in the wild today, of which four are regarded as endangered. The *Asiatic or Indian lion* is preserved now only in a reserve in the Gir Forest in Gujarat, India.

Lions rest up in the midday sun.

Lions live in groups called prides composed of four to twelve females and their cubs which are born one to six in a litter. A pride is defended by one or two males and other males live alone or in bachelor prides. Pride territories, the boundaries of which are marked by roaring, urine marking (like domestic cats) and regular patrolling, can extend over as much as 400 sq. km. Sometimes adjacent territories overlap, but the central zone is always kept solely for the use of the 'home' pride. In the wild lions live for about 15 years, though in zoos and safari parks they often reach 20 years of age or more.

Lions have always borne the title 'Lord of the Jungle'. In fact this is nonsense. Firstly, lions generally live in open bush land and grassy savannahs, or even desert areas, not dense jungle. And, formidable big cats though they are, I don't regard them as being as mighty as the bigger, solitary and exceedingly aggressive tiger or the smaller, elusive leopard. Many of the old big game hunters regarded the leopard as the most dangerous of the large cats, and from my experience I'd go along with that.

Do not disturb

Lions, unlike tigers and leopards, usually hunt in pairs or groups, and, as we have seen, they have little stamina for the

Two lionesses and their cubs go out on the prowl.

chase. Occasionally, however, they do become 'man-eaters'. The Tsavo region of Kenya was once famous for its man-eating lions. At the turn of the century, dozens of people working to construct a railway line to the Indian Ocean were killed by several lions, two of which started the slaughter and accounted for most of the victims. When they were eventually shot, they turned out to be large males without manes. Some man-eater lions have been found to be diseased or incapacitated in some way, and they may have turned to human prey as being easy to catch, but many seem to be physically normal.

Nevertheless, the vast majority of lions one might come across in the wild are *not* aggressive towards man, but rather sleepy, retiring animals, except when hunting their normal prey – antelopes and zebra – when harassed or during the mating season. Lions sometimes tackle other animals. There is a report of a battle between two lions and a buffalo that lasted two hours, and in some areas they kill a fair number of giraffes, including adults. They will take on hippopotamus and occasionally young elephants. Adult elephants and rhinoceros can easily cope with lion attacks and are usually successful in protecting their young, provided the latter stay close to them.

★ ★ ★ ★ ★

'Have you ever seen a cross between a lion and a tiger, David?'

'Yes, several. I looked after one, a tigon – father a tiger, mum a lioness – at Belle Vue Zoo, Manchester for donkeys' years.'

'Do they occur in the wild?'

'No, and they never did. Tigons and ligers are always zoo-born, man-made creations.'

HIGH AND MIGHTY

We have sailed through a balmy star-sprinkled night with the radio providing a succession of appropriate musical accompaniments. While the hare in the full moon (look up and you will see him) watched over us, we travelled on a flower-perfumed breeze. You checked our course with the luminous compass while I made a broth of the mushrooms and wild garlic we had picked after hippo-hunting.

Thank goodness you saw the black outline of the rocks looming towards us.

'Collision!' you shout. I strike the gas control lever with all my might. The flames roar in even greater protest. The thud as the basket strikes ground is less than I had feared. Our container lurches violently threatening to spill us both out. Then we swing level again. The air bears us up once more.

'A close shave,' you mutter, pulling yourself up to the basket side and looking over. The lump of unexpected ground is disappearing behind us.

'A mountain top,' I reply; the impact has dislodged my tweed cap and my head feels cold in the icy air. Scanning the maps by torchlight I recognise the peak over which we have just scraped. Time to put down. Soon it will be dawn and the

This is what long necks are for. A male giraffe can reach to the top of the trees.

Daybreak and the giraffes are already browsing.

eastern horizon is already paling. Ten minutes later we are on terra firma in a clearing surrounded by dimly visible acacia trees.

'Look! Something's moving over there and I can hear it. A tree – it's a tree moving!' you gasp. Sure enough a tree does seem to be passing slowly from right to left in front of us, and there is another.

'Where are we, David?' You sound slightly apprehensive.

'Don't worry, those aren't the moving trees that frightened Shakespeare's Macbeth,' I reassure you. 'They're not trees at all. Look again.' The tall 'trunks' can be seen more clearly now.

'*Giraffes!*' you exclaim. 'Moving through the trees and feeding. So this is our next mighty animal. Do they always feed by night?'

'Giraffes dine for over twelve hours every day, mainly in the twilight, at dawn and dusk, but if there is plenty of moonlight, they adore midnight snacks too.'

As the dawn begins to break, the towering animals browsing in front of us begin to gain colour and their features are steadily revealed. The *high* and mighty animals that we are watching were once called camelopards because they were said to be a cross between a camel and a leopard.

Altitude problems

The giraffe is all legs and neck, far and away the tallest animal on earth. But why? What is the point of being apparently so gawky? In fact, the giraffe is not gawky at all. It gallops with surprising grace and speed, and it can defend itself with powerful well aimed kicks of those heavy-hoofed legs against its principal enemy, the lion, and against hyenas, leopards and hunting dogs which sometimes attack baby giraffes. I was once nearly killed by a bull giraffe that swiped at me with a forefoot. Having such great height is an advantage, firstly in enabling the animal to browse on foliage that is out of reach of other herbivorous animals, and secondly in providing a built-in watch-tower-like ability to spot danger far off.

The giraffe's mouth is equipped to deal with prickly leaves and twigs.

On average, big bull giraffes stand 4.5-5.0 m high from the ground to the tips of their peg-like 'horns', but heights of almost 6 m (over 1 m taller than a London double decker bus!) have been recorded. Giraffes have no very long-necked relatives alive today. Their closest living relative is the beautiful, rare and velvet-brown skinned *okapi*, which has a couple of giraffe-like pegs on the head of the male, a longish neck and some light patterning on the legs.

Our own neck, which is only a few centimetres long, has seven bones. So the neck of a giraffe, measuring 2-3 m, must surely contain many more – 50 might be a fair guess. Surprisingly, however, the number is the same – seven. But the giraffe's seven neck bones are very long and heavy.

In order to pump the blood up to the brain of such a tall animal, you might think that the giraffe's heart must be exceptionally big and powerful. In fact it is no bigger than that of a domestic cow. But it does have a curious system of one-way valves in the arteries of the neck to help the blood keep moving up when the animal is standing normally, and to stop blood rushing to the brain when the head is down for drinking. Some years ago I was the first person to measure the blood pressure of a calm, untranquillised, normal giraffe. Oddly, this too isn't much higher than that of a cow.

View from the top

Giraffes are ruminants, cud-chewing animals like cows, but unlike most of these, they are born with horns. The horns, still rather rubbery, lie flat on the head of a newborn baby giraffe, but stand up by the end of the first week of life. They are browsers, loving the leaves and shoots of bushes and trees, particularly those of acacias. It's easy to tell the sex of a giraffe at a distance by observing the way they browse. Male giraffes stretch their necks high up into the trees to eat, while female giraffes arch their necks over to eat foliage lower down. They can easily cope with thorny plants, being equipped with heavily grooved and thickened roofs to their mouths and by producing large quantities of thick saliva that protects the softer parts like the tongue. Giraffes and okapis both have a long, mobile, grey-black tongue which they use to curl round twigs and bunches of leaves which are then plucked off. A giraffe tongue can shoot out as far as 50 cm. The giraffe's front teeth are broad and splayed, with lobed canine (fang) teeth specially for stripping leaves off branches. There are no teeth at the front of the upper jaw – just a hard pad that the lower front teeth bite against when neatly breaking off non-spiky shoots and leaves.

Apart from the lion, the giraffe's principal enemy is man. Some African tribes, particularly in the Sudan, Chad and Ethiopia, have traditionally hunted it, sometimes on horseback, as a source of meat. But the giraffe has also been killed just to take the tail hairs to make bracelets for tourists. The tuft of tail hair serves the giraffe as an efficient fly whisk.

The giraffe has excellent senses of smell, hearing and sight. Its vision is particularly acute. It can detect small movement at a distance of 3 km, and the field of vision is wider than a cinemascope screen, covering almost 270 degrees, thanks

A vulnerable moment for this giraffe as it splays its legs to lick bones on the ground.

largely to the eye's horizontal letterbox-shaped pupil (not round as in the human eye). The animal's height enables it to act as a living watchtower – that is why other creatures such as cattle and wildebeest like to graze near by. Their long-necked friends act as early-warning devices, detecting the approach of predators. Giraffes are at their most vulnerable when they are drinking. To get their head down to the water, they must splay their legs, and lions like to launch their attacks at such moments. Very sensibly, one or two giraffes always act as sentries with their heads held high when the others are drinking.

Coats of all patterns

Giraffe mothers undergo a pregnancy of about 15 months. The females give birth in giraffe 'maternity hospitals', the same calving grounds that are used year after year. One female may give birth to a dozen babies during her lifetime, although about half of all giraffe calves die during the first six months of life. The mothers often leave groups of calves alone while they go off to feed themselves during the heat of the middle of the day. They know that the lions find it too hot to go out hunting and prefer to lie snoozing at this time, but they are careful to return to guard their offspring when the temperature begins to drop in the late afternoon.

There are generally believed to be nine (although some people say as many as 20) subspecies of giraffe, identifiable by their variations in basic coat pattern. Every individual giraffe has its own unique and

A giraffe calf suckles from its mother.

personal coat pattern that it shares with no other individual. All giraffes live in the savannahs and open woodlands of Africa south of the Sahara Desert. Once they could be found right up to the Mediterranean coastline of North Africa and across to the Atlantic coast in the west. They are not, as a species, endangered, though some subspecies, such as *Rothschild's giraffe* of western Kenya, occur now in only small numbers. Giraffe herds are usually composed of females and youngsters, although there are a few bachelor herds. Bulls tend to live alone.

* * * * *

'How fast can a giraffe run?' you ask.

'Up to about 65 kmh, and when they do gallop, the hind legs come forwards and are set down more or less at the same time, outside the forelegs. A thrilling sight.'

'If this is Africa and those are giraffes, what was that mountain top we skimmed?'

'Kilimanjaro – we're in Tanzanian territory.'

'And where do we go next?'

'Nowhere – till we've had breakfast. Watching all those giraffes chomping the foliage has made me quite hungry.'

Some of the different giraffe markings.

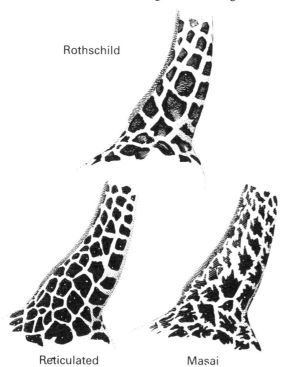

Rothschild

Reticulated   Masai

JUNGLE VICTIM

et down! Prepare for a rough landing!' I bark out the words as we skim over the trees. There is a sharp crackling sound as the basket touches the topmost branches. Sweating, for it is a furnace-hot, humid afternoon, you grab one of the safety ropes and squat on your haunches. I notice your right-hand fingers are crossed.

KERRASH! Somehow the basket stays more or less upright as we plunge through the tree cover and come to a bumpy halt in a bed of young bamboo. Vine leaves flutter down like confetti and the balloon settles gently over us. There is the smell of sandalwood and damp vegetation. Cicadas thrum steadily and invisibly in the trees. A green snake flicks its tongue at

What on earth is this rhino doing in a hole?

one of our ropes impinging on its resting place, coiled around a branch. Far away, perhaps alarmed by our noisy landfall, monkeys hoot.

There are other noises too, coming from near by. A dull thudding, the heavy crunching of vegetation under foot, husky breathing and the occasional deep grunt. We climb warily out of the basket and I lead the way, pressing apart the bamboo and tall grass.

It's hard going in the dense undergrowth, but I don't want to use the machete I've brought along, until we know what it is that is making the noises.

Beyond a jumble of rotting fallen tree trunks coated in bright green moss, we find ourselves standing in a more open space. To right and left an indistinct trail runs through the trees. Bushes have been

broken down, undergrowth trodden into a damp carpet – it is some sort of pathway, but surely not man-made.

'Our next mighty animal is somewhere around,' I say, wiping the streams of stinging sweat from my face. 'Come on, let's turn right and follow its highway.'

'But David, it's quite narrow – what if we come face to face with whatever it is – coming the other way?'

'Say a prayer to St Francis,' I reply, 'but don't worry – it's a strict vegetarian and wouldn't fancy eating you!'

A Sumatran rhino at home in the jungle.

We have walked barely 100 m when I stop. 'Look!' I say. In front of us a large rectangular hole yawns in the pathway. The thudding, crunching, grunting noises are loud now – and they are coming from the hole!

'What on earth is it?' you whisper. Then, 'I know – a giant armadillo digging into the earth – we're in South America!'

'Wrong – we're far away from there. This is the Far East, a land, actually an archipelago, comprising over 3,000 islands and part of what was once the Dutch East Indies.'

'I give up,' you reply, 'but let me *please* look into the hole!' We move slowly forwards and peep over the edge. At the

bottom of a 2 m deep pit cut into the earth with vertical sides stands a stocky animal, perhaps 3 m long, that bears two short horns on its snout and is covered all over with coarse reddish hair. A *rhinoceros*. But a very special, very rare rhinoceros. From time to time he rams his muscle into the black earth wall that faces him. He grunts in frustration, paws the ground beneath him and rolls bloodshot eyes.

'How are the mighty fallen! This my young friend is a *Sumatran rhino* – which makes sense, because we are on the island of Sumatra.'

'What's he doing in a hole?'

'The hole is a pit-fall, a trap dug by poachers in one of the pathways made and used regularly by rhinos as they travel through their jungle territory. It would have been camouflaged by the branches and leaves that he's now standing upon.'

'But why? Do they mean to eat him?'

'No – they want just two things – his horns. The stumps of compressed hair, for that is what rhino horn is composed of, which he carries on his nose. In the Orient such rhino horns – it doesn't matter whether they come from Sumatran, *white* or *black rhino* – are greatly prized as being of medicinal value, especially for love potions. Just one good horn can command a price of $30,000!'

'And is it a good medicine?'

'Much of traditional Far Eastern medicine, using all sorts of vegetable and animal products, is effective, and we in the West can learn a lot from it, but we know *for sure* that rhino horn is of no value at all – except to its rightful owner, the rhino!'

'So what are we going to do? Let the poor beast stay in the hole and then be killed just so some fellow can steal its horns?'

'Definitely not – we'll do something.' I take my machete out of its canvas sheath. 'I'll start cutting branches. You carry them to the pit and throw them in. Gradually we'll fill it up so that the rhino's "floor" is raised. It might take us all day –

Mud glorious mud! A Sumatran rhino relishes its wallow.

but if we can do it, eventually he'll be level with the ground and can then escape.'

'Fan-tastic!' you shout. 'Let's get at it!'

By nightfall I am absolutely exhausted. The rhino, stamping about, has trodden down and compacted the bundles of branches you have thrown around him. Now his feet are almost at ground height. Just as you throw in yet another bundle, he suddenly scrambles up the remaining half metre of earth, gives a mighty grunt, and without a glance in our direction, dashes off into the jungle.

'HOORAY!' you bellow – I don't know where you get the energy from. 'He's safe!'

'Thank blooming goodness,' I sigh. 'My arms feel like rubber bands!'

Danger signs

There are five species of rhino alive today. The one in the hole is the smallest, one of the rarest, and, to my mind because of its red hair, the oddest. It is the Sumatran rhino which weighs up to about 800 kg. Only a few hundred such animals, scattered about the jungles, are left alive. The *Javan rhino* is even more endangered, with a world population totalling no more than 50 animals. The black rhino and the white rhino are inhabitants of Africa; and the mightiest of the lot, the *great Indian rhinoceros*, can weigh 2 tonnes and may grow a horn 60 cm in length. It has the most armour-plated look of all the rhinoceros family, and was the one that the great early sixteenth-century artist, Dürer, drew as a wondrous armoured beast. (He, like most Europeans, had never seen a rhinoceros, but only received

A white rhino mother with her calf in South Africa.

descriptions and a sketch from travellers.)

But imagine, 30 million years ago there was a much bigger rhino trundling around Europe and Asia. It was hornless, measured about 11 m long, including its rather long neck, and weighed up to 20 tonnes, a little more than three modern bull elephants! You could have driven a station wagon between its fore and hind legs without the vehicle's roof touching its tummy. That rhino, called *Baluchitherium*, was the largest land mammal that has ever lived. There were many different kinds of rhino all over the earth at one time, with a *woolly rhino* surviving in Europe until about 15,000 years ago.

The fateful horn

The name rhinoceros means literally in Greek 'nose horn'. Rhinos are vegetarians who eat large quantities of plant food. They are very short-sighted, but have an excellent sense of hearing, through those swivelling sound-funnelling ears, and absolutely brilliant powers of smell.

They can reach an age of 40 years or more and tend to live solitary lives except for the females who keep their babies with them until the next one is born. The most friendly of all rhinos is the white rhino – it sometimes forms pairs or bigger groups, up to six or seven, of immature animals. In zoos and safari parks, white rhinos often become as docile and amenable towards their human acquaintances as domestic cattle. The black is much more aggressive. When a rhino charges, it puts its head down and simply goes – guided by sound and smell. It doesn't *look* its target in the eye. Although most of the charges are bluff, simply to frighten the person or animal away, humans who get too close or annoy the animal too much can get into serious trouble.

In nature rhinos don't have any enemies except man, and all because of that horn. As well as for making medicines, men take the horn to make dagger handles which sell for very high prices in Arabia. And there were other uses in days gone by. It was long believed that if a suspect liquid were put into a cup made of rhino horn, it would bubble if it were poisonous.

UNDERWATER ELEPHANT

*I*t is atrocious weather. The unrelenting wind, driving heavy rain before it, has forced us to land. What a desolate place – black, scoured rocks running as far as the eye can see against the mist of rain, patches of brown, wiry grass like mould on the land, and here and there encrustations of moss brittle with ice.

'When the rain stops we'll go to the cliff edge over there and mount a watch on the sea.'

'For a mighty marine monster?' you ask.

'Right. The mightiest animal of its kind.'

'Then it must be – I know – a whale!'

'No. But here's a clue. 'What lives in a rookery?'

'Rooks!'

'Yes, but also something else. Rookery is the name given to the home, on land, of a group of pinnipeds, 'fin-footed' mammals such as seals and sealions.'

'So we're here to see a seal rookery!'

'Exactly – just over the cliff edge is a pebbly beach that happens to be the rookery of a herd of elephants.'

On a cold and windy Patagonian beach, elephant seals are well insulated by their fat.

'Hah!' you guffaw, 'you're teasing me, David – or the crab meat you've just eaten for lunch is off and giving you hallucinations.'

I chuckle and huddle closer to the fire. 'No, they are often called elephants – sea elephants. We are going to watch the giant among seals, the *elephant seal* – a monster that can weigh over 2 tonnes!'

We stagger over the gleaming black rocks to the cliff edge and, swaddled in extra layers of sweaters and waterproofs, look down to the shoreline. The sea is black and boiling, exploding where it rolls against the dark beach into startling white eruptions of foam.

There on the beach are what we have come to see. Dozens of black-brown roly-poly sausages – enormous, plump seals, wobbly and ungainly and bulging with fat as they haul themselves along almost caterpillar-fashion.

'Sea elephants!' you cry against the howling wind. 'But how can they live in such a freezing, unfriendly place? Where are we anyway?'

'This is Tierra del Fuego, the "Land of Fire", at the southern tip of the South American continent. The first Portuguese explorers of the region gave it that name when they saw the many signal fires lit by

A bull elephant seal seems surprisingly proud of his grotesque 'hooter'!

the local Indians as a warning against the "big canoes" of the Europeans. Out there is the south Atlantic, the treacherous seas around Cape Horn and cold water all the way down to Antarctica. Inhospitable to man, but great for elephant seals.'

As we watch, more elephant seals arrive through the breakers and haul out on to the beach, briefly glistening with water.

Suddenly you yell, 'Look, David, a shark – cutting in towards the beach!' I see the triangular dorsal fin slicing through the waves. Black, almost a metre high, the sinister triangle is making straight for a young elephant seal at the water's edge. But it isn't a shark.

'*Killer whale!*' I shout, and at that moment the black and white body below the fin breaks through the surface. There's a flash of pink, a gleam of ivory teeth, as a great mouth opens. Too late, the elephant seal lumbers for the beach. Half-grounded itself, the killer whale's jaws clamp down on the seal's trunk and a patch of red blooms in the water. The whale arches its spine and backs off into

the next incoming breaker, taking its luckless prey with it. It has all happened in just a few seconds. Stunned, you turn to stare at me. 'Does that often happen?' you ask.

'Quite often. Apart from man, quite recently, the elephant seal has only two natural enemies – the killer whale and the great white shark. And it is virtually defenceless against them.'

Unlikely athletes

Male elephant seals may reach a length of 6 m and females 3 m, with waist measurements of up to 3.5 m. These huge animals are ungainly, almost ridiculously clumsy, on land (quite a number of seal pups are squashed to death by adults as they heave themselves about on the beaches), but don't be deceived. Their bodies are superbly designed and efficient for life in deep, dark, cold water where they spend the majority of their time. Lacking, like all true seals, external ears, and with smooth, rounded bodies, they are streamlined for cutting through the water. They propel themselves by means of the hind flippers (unlike sealions who 'row' through the water with their fore flippers) and keep the front limbs tucked into the body to reduce water resistance or use them as rudders to help steering.

In the sea, therefore, these animals are amazingly agile and athletic. Even chimps and cheetahs do not possess a backbone as flexible as that of an elephant seal, which can bend over *backwards* to form a 35 degree V shape. Beneath the skin is a thick layer of special, semi-liquid, fat (blubber) which is both an insulator against the cold and a store of food.

Elephant seals are superb divers, able to go down to at least 650 m and stay under for half an hour, hunting the fish, squid and crabs on which they feed. To go so deep for so long they conserve oxygen in their bodies by slowing their heart beats and, by shutting down certain blood vessels, divert oxygen-rich blood to essential organs such as brain and heart. They

can carry down extra oxygen due to the fact that they have 50 per cent more blood, weight for weight, than a human being, and more of an oxygen-storing chemical called myoglobin in their muscles.

Down in the dark depths of the sea, they locate their prey thanks to large eyes with a pupil that dilates enormously in poor light. Behind the light-sensitive retina of the eye is a 'mirror' of special cells that concentrates any available light, and the lens of the eye is ball-shaped (unlike yours which is an ovoid disc) which enables the seal to focus sharply below the surface. They can also hear well under water, detect pressure changes through their sensitive whiskers and, perhaps, a bit like dolphins, employ an echo-location (sonar) system.

Harems and pups

There are two species of elephant seal, the *Northern elephant seal*, which breeds on the Californian and Mexican coasts, and

Two bull elephant seals do battle in the surf.

A mother elephant seal and her baby on the beach.

the *Southern elephant seal*, whose rookeries are situated in the southern tip of South America, Antarctica, the Falkland Islands and a number of other islands in the southern hemisphere. Like the other true (earless) seals, elephant seals evolved from the primitive weasel family group about 14 million years ago (whereas sealions and the other eared seals branched off from the bear's family tree).

Elephant seal society is organised on a 'harem' system with a group of females, perhaps as many as 50 animals, being mated and protected by a dominant bull. Elephant seal pups on the Californian coast are born, beginning in late December, about one week after their mothers arrive on land. The pup weighs around 30 kg. The mother suckles the infant on a very rich milk for one month, during which time its weight triples. Most pups are weaned by early March and the adults then mate and return to the ocean. The youngsters spend their days on land

and practise swimming skills at sea during the night. At the end of March, they also set out to sea and, unless ill or injured, don't return to land for just over a year.

Once, elephant seals were greatly threatened by man who hunted them for their oil. By the beginning of this century the number of Northern elephant seals had been reduced to about 100. Now, thanks to conservation efforts and the end of hunting, this species flourishes once again and may number over 100,000.

★ ★ ★ ★ ★

'What incredible animals!' you say. 'Do you think I can get closer to take some photographs?'

'Sure. I suggest you put on your wetsuit and then go down to the rookery and wriggle across the pebbles on your tummy. You'll look like a small and unimportant black seal – of no interest or threat to anybody. Then you'll get your close-ups.'

LEVIATHAN

'*T*ierra del Fuego was bad, but this is even worse,' you groan, picking at a crust of ice that has formed on the basket rim. We are both wearing our parkas and woollen gloves, and though our faces glow in the light of the burners, they feel numb with the bitter cold. The balloon is travelling slowly on a level course through thin patches of cloud laced with sleet. When we emerge briefly from a cloud, we can see only grey heaving ocean beneath us.

'Hot Bovril and a bacon sandwich coming up,' I reply, trying to sound cheerful as I fumble with the primus stove. 'We are pretty sure to sight our next mighty animal any time now.'

'So we'll see land soon?'

'Not today, I fear.'

You scowl briefly, but then your red face breaks into a smile. 'So it's another mighty sea animal?'

'Yes. The mightiest beast alive on earth.'

'Then it must be – I know – a *whale*!'

'Correct. It is a whale that can grow as long as 30 m and weigh up to 160 tonnes, including a 3 tonne tongue. How many kinds of whale do you know of?'

'Er – over 40, I think. The *sperm*, the *humpback*, the *fin*, the *sei*, the *pilot*, the *killer*, the *beluga*, the . . . '

'And the greatest of them all?' I interrupt.

'The *blue whale*!'

'Right again. We're on course over the South Atlantic, about 300 km off the island of South Georgia.'

'Ship ahoy! Look, there's a ship down there. I'll see if I can identify its flag – yes, there it is. White with a red disc in the centre. Japanese!'

It is indeed a Japanese vessel. I watch it riding through the rolling sea, black hull, white superstructure stained with rust, funnel belching blue smoke and a bulky mast with a crow's nest look-out at the top.

The impressive form of a humpback whale underwater.

'It's a whaler,' I murmur. 'The thing on the bows is the harpoon gun and its platform. I suspect they're after our mighty beast, too!'

'Whalers!' you gasp. 'But I thought whaling had been stopped.'

'Not completely. Some countries, in particular Japan and Iceland, still take a number of whales each year for so-called scientific research purposes.'

'And do they kill blue whales?'

'They're not supposed to – let's drop down below the cloud level and see where that boat is heading.'

Forty metres above the waves we survey the vast monochrome sheet of the ocean that laps Antarctica. All is grey – sea and sky. The Japanese ship is steaming along directly below us. You spot the whale first. A plume of vapour, the 'blow', ascends as the gigantic animal breaks the surface to exhale. Barely a dozen metres from the whaler's bow we see a silvery grey expanse of skin, a double-nostrilled blow-hole and the shadow of an immense body perhaps 20 m long. It is undoubtedly our quarry – a blue whale – the mightiest animal in the ocean.

On board the whaler there is much activity. The man in the crow's nest is speaking animatedly into a hand-held microphone. Two other men are running down a sort of catwalk to the harpoon platform. One takes his place behind the harpoon gun. We can see him swivelling it.

'He's aiming for the whale!' you exclaim. 'But aren't blue whales protected?'

'They are – but sometimes, disgracefully, the rules are broken. Once it's been killed and processed on board the mother ship, a sort of floating butcher's shop, who's to say it ever was a blue whale, and not, say, a fin or sei whale?'

You growl angrily. 'Can't we do something – can't we . . .? Then, on a sudden impulse, you grab one of the smoke flares we carry for emergencies, pull the tab and at once the dense red smoke begins to billow out. 'What the . . . ?' I gasp. Lean-

Caught in the act! A Japanese whaler prepares to harpoon a blue whale.

A blue whale blows (exhales).

ing over the basket side you hurl the flare down towards the harpooner who is still taking aim with the gun that in a moment will send a lump of explosive-containing steel deep into the body of his prey. Well aimed! The flare lands close to the base of the gun mount and the harpooner is at once enveloped in a choking crimson cloud of smoke.

Meanwhile, gloriously, the blue whale has indeed dived – for the moment at least it is safe, perhaps a kilometre down – and it can stay down for a long, long time.

'Time to go,' I say, turning up the burners. 'We'd better get back into the cloud out of range of that pistol.' Moments later we are high in the cold grey mist, unable to see or be seen.

The biggest ever

The blue whale is the largest animal that has ever lived on this planet. Like all whales and dolphins, however, and although it lives its life completely in the sea, it has evolved from a land animal. It is a baleen whale, a member of the group of whales without teeth which sift their food from the sea water by means of baleen (whalebone) plates, rather like rows of bristles, set in the mouth. Some other whales, such as the sperm and killer, along with all dolphins and porpoises have teeth. Blue whales feed almost exclusively on krill, shrimp-like

A mother killer whale and her calf.

creatures that abound in the oceans, particularly where the water is cold and rich in oxygen.

Blue whales spend the summer of the southern hemisphere feeding close to the edge of the Antarctic ice. Then they migrate north for thousands of kilometres over well-known routes to reach breeding grounds in the Indian Ocean. Where these are exactly we still don't know. As they go the whales communicate with one another by underwater sounds that can travel over 5,000 km and they navigate perhaps by having the ability to sense the earth's magnetic field much in the way that pigeons can. They do not appear to be able to echo-locate (use sonar) like toothed whales and dolphins.

Pregnancy in a female blue whale lasts one year and the single 7 m long calf is suckled on milk far richer than any cow's, for six to seven months. A blue whale can live for as long as 80 years. These warm-blooded, air-breathing mammals were hunted almost to extinction by man. Where once, before commercial whaling began, there had been over 200,000 of them in the Southern Ocean alone, by the late 1970s perhaps only 7,000 blue whales remained in the whole world. Today they are, theoretically, protected from whaling, though pollution of the oceans may pose a serious future threat. Their numbers seem slowly to be increasing, but they are still an endangered species. It would be immensely sad if these mighty, harmless and very beautiful creatures were to disappear for good.

CHEQUERBOARD MONSTER

A wild night of screaming winds that toss the balloon around the sky; we have touched the outer edge of the first of the season's hurricanes. Morning dawns on a troubled ocean, blue-black with ranks of frothy breakers on the march as far as the eye can see. To the west sullen clouds, the storm's rearguard, reach down to the water, and in the east a silvery sun rises through the mist, softly illuminating the sandy shoreline that we can see perhaps 20 km away and 700 m below us. There is little noise now, just the familiar creak of the basket. The burners are off.

While you heat some coffee over the stove, I assemble the scuba gear and the inflatable dinghy.

The whale shark is the biggest and yet the gentlest fish in the sea.

'We'll land on the beach right ahead.' I point towards the coast that bristles beyond the sand with the tallest palm trees, rising to 30 m or more, that we have ever seen.

'And where might we be?' you ask as you hand me a steaming mug. 'The Caribbean?'

'Yes. And that is the island of Cuba, the beach at Varadero, to be precise.'

'Ah! So the diving gear must mean we're after some great sea beast of the warmer oceans!' You grin triumphantly.

'A great sea beast for sure – one of the biggest, gentlest, most mysterious and most beautiful,' I reply.

'Give me a clue.'

'Harmless, very rarely seen by man, attractively spotted and as long, perhaps, as two double decker buses.'

'The great sea serpent!'

'No – but enough of the questions, *amigo*, prepare for landing – and don't forget your waterproof camera. With any luck you'll get a snap of the animal that the Cubans call "chequerboard." '

Before you can ask any more questions I turn away to the control cables and set about commencing our descent. Forty minutes later, with the balloon and its basket securely lashed down, we pull the dinghy across the sand and set out on to the rolling sea. Ten kilometres out we throw overboard a sea anchor, strap on the air tanks, flippers, weight belts, and other equipment, and tumble backwards from the dinghy's side into the water.

Five metres beneath the surface it is a still, blue-green, crystal-clear world peopled by shoals of metallic-gleaming coloured fish that move in synchronised drills. We wait hanging in the water. Then I tap your shoulder and point.

Slowly, out of the infinite blue, a shape emerges. It appears to fill the sea. A submarine? No. This is something *alive*. Silently it approaches and we find ourselves face to face with a monster 20 m in length and weighing perhaps as much as 40 tonnes. We are extraordinarily lucky to come across such a beast for, since it was first identified by scientists about 160 years ago, it has only been seen by human eyes about once every 18 months on average; in total, therefore, a mere 115 times. And yet, you and I are in no danger. This is a benign, harmless animal and although it is the giant of its kind, it

doesn't have a single bone in its body!

Looking at the massive face from the front, we get a rather frog-like impression, produced by the broad mouth that runs all the way across the snout. Small eyes are set low at the sides of the head. We paddle back as the creature travels sedately on, and thrill to the attractive appearance of its skin.

Beneath, it is a yellowish-white, but the sides and top are grey-brown decorated with a regular grid-pattern of pale lines and a heavy sprinkling of circular yellow spots. With the lines of the grid being evenly spaced and enclosing the spots, the animal's side does indeed remind us of a game of draughts; now we understand why the Cubans call it the 'chequerboard'.

A docile giant

The animal passing before us is the biggest fish in the world, the very rare and little known *whale shark*. Like all sharks, it is a member of a class of fish regarded by scientists as somewhat more ancient and primitive than 'modern' bony fish such as the cod, stickleback and salmon. Sharks have a skeleton that is built, not of bone, but of cartilage, the stuff that forms the framework of our nose and ear flaps. The whale shark has a more humped back than other sharks. Its dorsal fin is rounded and set well down the back. The tail is huge, and from top to bottom tip generally measures about one-quarter the length of the body.

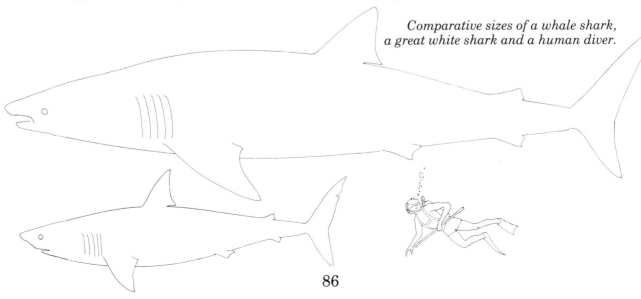

Comparative sizes of a whale shark, a great white shark and a human diver.

So if it's a shark, isn't there a risk of it being a man-eater? After all, the *great white shark* reaches only about 6 m in length and has a fearsome reputation – and this living submarine is over three times as long! No, the whale shark is only interested in feeding on plankton, that teeming broth of the oceans which is composed of microscopic marine life, tiny shrimps and squid, and shoals of little fish. Rather like the baleen or whalebone whales, it gulps down vast mouthfuls of water containing these creatures, clamps shut its jaws that bristle with about 7,000 tiny, spiked teeth, and pumps out the water through its gill-slits. The plankton is sieved out and retained as the water exits by brush-like filters called gill-rakers. It is then swallowed down a rather narrow gullet that has a dog-leg turn in it to prevent the accidental intake of any large items.

Again like the plankton-eating whales, whale sharks need vast quantities of plankton to keep their appetites satisfied. They have normally been seen in a band of tropical waters that extend to about 4,000 km north and south of the equator. Very rarely 'strays' have gone as far north as waters off New York, USA, but the majority of the still few and scattered

A rare photograph – the gigantic whale shark is seldom seen.

sightings of this wonderful fish have been in areas such as the Florida Straits, the Caribbean and the Philippines.

Whale sharks easily hold the size record for fish – the smallest one ever measured was nearly 2 m long, and we have no idea how big the babies are at birth. Very little is known about the life-style of this peaceful leviathan – where does it wander? How long can it live? How big can it grow? Are the babies born alive or in egg-cases?

The whale shark has the amiable temperament of a large dog such as a labrador. Although it never attacks humans, it has upset fishing boats by accidentally brushing against or rising beneath them, for it spends much time basking at the surface. Philippine fishermen dislike it, because of its habit of ruining nets as it blunders on its way.

Now, apparently paying us no attention whatever, our whale shark glides away, its 5 m high tail moving slowly from side to side. Soon it disappears, swallowed by the distant gloom. I wonder when the next sighting of a whale shark will occur. Meanwhile, let's get back to the balloon!

HERO OF THE WESTERNS

I don't like the look of it! The burners are on full power, but we are losing height. When we flew through a skein of geese just after daybreak, one of them collided violently with the balloon – we must have suffered a rip in the fabric with consequent loss of hot air. No matter, we'll land now.

You are peering through the binoculars at a small collection of wooden houses set in the middle of nowhere. Sagging roofs, doors reeling away from broken hinges, bleached shingles and the rusting remains of a water tower. There is no sign of life in the ghost town. Burners off, make some calculations of wind speed and altitude – with any luck we'll be down on that patch of brown hillside. Must avoid the pillars of rock.

'I've arranged by radio for a friend to meet us with a jeep when we land.'

'But where are we?'

Before I can answer, we bump down and both of us set about the routine task of pulling in the deflating balloon. All around us is rolling grassland, with here and there tall fingers of white rock rising

Echoes of cowboys and Indians – fortunately the buffalo still roam the American plains.

from the plain and some miles away a line of jagged mountains, the colour of rich cream in the sunlight.

'Look!' you shout, pointing, 'What a monster!'

From behind a soaring pillar of weather beaten sandstone 100 m away, a massive brown-black figure moves into view. The large head is held close to the ground as it feeds. The curved horns shine. It is a *buffalo*. Then we see another and another. There must be a dozen or more, all quietly grazing. A trio of beardless chestnut calves interrupt their play to stare in our direction.

Slaughter on the prairie

This is Montana USA, a part of the Great Plains area that encompasses the lands east of the Rocky Mountains from the Canadian border to the mouth of the Arkansas river. Once, enormous herds of these mighty members of the wild cattle family roamed the prairies of this land, and for thousands of years were the chief attraction for the tribesmen who came to live here. Great buffalo-hunting Indian tribes such as the Dakota, Arapaho, Cheyenne, Kiowa, Apache and Comanche, were completely dependent on the

The dangerous African buffalo surrounded by a group of egret admirers.

animals that provided meat for food, horn and bone for implements and skins for leather. Later, with the coming of the horse, firearms and European explorers, the region became peopled largely by roving bands of buffalo hunters. You know the old song, 'Oh give me a home where the buffalo roam, where the deer and the antelope play.'

Where once the buffaloes of the American plains numbered perhaps as many as 50 million, the great herds declined drastically in the nineteenth century as the Wild West was settled by the white men. They hunted the buffalo not only for its commercial value, but also as a means of suppressing the Indians who depended on it for survival. By 1895 only about 800 buffalo were left in the whole of North America and most of them were in Canada. One of the most famous buffalo hunters was William F. Cody, 'Buffalo

Bill', who got his name by supplying the men building the Kansas Pacific railway through the wilderness with buffalo meat. He later served in the US 5th Cavalry and killed the Cheyenne chief, Yellow Hand, in single combat. Buffalo Bill died in Denver, Colorado, just over 70 years ago.

It's good to know that conservation programmes, including the setting up of protected reserves such as the Yellowstone National Park, have saved the American buffalo from extinction, and its numbers have risen again to over 50,000. Actually, the famous American buffalo, so often seen stampeding through cowboy films, is more correctly called the *American bison*. It isn't the same as the *water buffalo* of Asia which, domesticated, is to be found also in South America, North Africa and even parts of Europe such as Italy. Nor is it to be confused with the *African buffaloes* which President Theodore Roosevelt, a keen big game hunter, correctly described as 'tough animals, tenacious of life

and among the most dangerous of African game'.

No, the American bison (buffalo) is a different, even more spectacular animal, though it has a close relative, the *European bison* or *wisent*, living in Europe. The latter once roamed over much of Europe, and prehistoric wall paintings of them, some up to 30,000 years old, have been found in caves in Spain, France, Italy and Russia. They too were hunted and by the beginning of this century were reduced to a small herd in the Bialowiecza Forest in Poland and another in the Russian Caucasus. By 1925 they were extinct in the wild. Luckily, re-establishment of the wisent was possible using animals existing in zoos, and today they again roam the wooded lands of Poland and Russia where they are strictly protected.

Dust of battle

The American bison is rather larger and has longer hair on its head and shoulders than the European kind, but otherwise they are very similar in appearance and it may be that they are both subspecies of the bison species. Two kinds of American bison are recognised, the *southern plains bison* and the somewhat darker and larger *wood buffalo* that lives farther north. In 1959 a previously unknown herd of pure wood bison was discovered in Alberta, Canada.

Of all the cattle family, the bison are undoubtedly the mightiest, at least in appearance. Tall and heavy, with a noble, shaggy, bearded head set on powerful forequarters that rise to an impressive hump at the withers, they are imposing animals, particularly when viewed head on. Adult American bison males weigh about 1 tonne and females about 500 kg, but much heavier specimens of as much as 1½ tonnes are on record. The bull bison, nearly twice as big as the female, is a

A buffalo enjoys a dust bath in the afternoon.

The ritual fighting of two American buffalo bulls.

picture of power, an animal whose sole function in life is to challenge and fight other males for the right to mate with cows during the breeding season. Nothing in the world of wildlife is more spectacular than the battling of two bison bulls as they go through their warlike rituals, threatening by swinging their heads up and down, often in unison, bellowing, rolling in the dust and, if one of the pair doesn't give in and move away after all this theatricality, clashing with loud thuds, head against head, vicious horns grinding together and hooves raking the ground. Such contests for the favours of the cows sometimes result in bloody wounds or, less frequently, death. But, as in other species, bison bulls spend more time mock-fighting and trying to intimidate one another, often with great success, than in serious combat. Only about one in seven confrontations end in the gladiators locking horns.

Bison live in groups of 10-20 animals, which merge into much larger herds in the breeding season, July to September.

After a pregnancy of approximately nine months, the cows give birth in April to June. Bison can interbreed with domestic cattle to produce 'cattalos'. In zoos bison can live for up to 25 years.

★ ★ ★ ★ ★

It's time to take a photograph of the buffalo as they slowly move along, grazing, before they disappear from sight. Then we must start inspecting every inch of the balloon fabric to find and patch the leak before we lift off to begin our long journey home. There's at least a week's flying to do before we can shut off the gas burner for the final time. Tell me – which of our ten mighty animals impressed you the most?'

You think for a few minutes, then you say 'I think it was the

. . . . '

(Fill in your own answer here)

ANIMALS IN BATTLE

FIGHTING MONSTERS FROM CARTHAGE

*I*magine. it is December in the year 218 BC, and you, a peasant lad from the hills near the ancient Etruscan city of Saena Julia (modern-day Sienna), have enlisted in the army of Rome. The legion to which you belong is camped in frosty, foggy weather on the banks of the River Trebia about 75 km south of the city we know nowadays as Milan.

It's a hard life – brutal discipline, long marches on a diet of boiled garlic and pickled fish, and bloody skirmishes with hostile tribespeople and Carthaginian patrols. Now, along with your comrades-in-arms of Wolf cohort (a cohort is one-tenth of a legion and comprises 600 men) you wait, trying to draw some warmth from the camp fires . . . waiting for the coming of the dreaded Hannibal, the mighty enemy general from Africa who recently crossed the Alps in a surprise invasion with 70,000 men. Rumours abound as the legionaries sit sharpening sword blades on hard stone and passing round the wine skin.

'This devil from Carthage, this Hannibal, fights not only with men and horses,' mutters your friend Gaius. 'They say he has terrible monsters too.'

'Hah, what nonsense,' retorts a soldier crouched on the other side of the fire. 'Women's tales. Now he's in Italy, the Carthaginian dog will face proper Roman steel, not those half-baked conscripts sent against him in Spain, nor those wild Gauls up north!'

You chuckle nervously and wonder what *will* happen when the armies clash.

This elephant charging at you through an African marsh, its ears spread wide, gives an idea of the effect experienced by a defending Roman soldier.

The scouts have brought news that the enemy will arrive tomorrow. They said nothing about monsters though.

During the night you sleep hardly at all under your goatskins. The damp chill penetrates your bones, some of the men sing noisily for hours and always there's the gnawing worry – Hannibal the invincible? Monsters?

Dawn breaks, with the land and the river shrouded in drizzling mist. Officers ride round the camp bellowing orders. There are trumpet calls echoing eerily, the trumpeters invisible in the haze. Standards are raised and men take up their accustomed positions in the battle lines. The smells of wood fires, horse dung, sweat, leather, garlic and wet grass hang in the dank air.

'The enemy is drawn up 500 paces away,' says the man who stands to your right, pointing the way with one of his throwing spears. 'Curse this fog, they'll be upon us before we can see them.'

An hour passes. Excitement and fear make you forget the cold. The Roman legion is by now in perfect order; the men,

A working Indian elephant effortlessly carries a tree trunk up a riverbank in Nepal.

clad in metal helmets and leather cuirasses have formed three lines. They are armed with large shields and short thrusting swords, with the addition of throwing spears in the front two lines and long spears in the third line. And they are ready for anything.

A distant trumpet blares. A chorus of voices gets steadily louder somewhere in the mist in front of you. More noises – of feet tramping, metal clanking, animals snorting – can be heard. The enemy approaches. You see shadows in the gloom, darkening, enlarging.

'Steady, lads!' your officer barks. 'Throw true and throw hard when I give the word!'

Spears jut like a hedge of iron thorns. Surely your line of armed and bristling men is impregnable. Then it happens – through the smoking, vapour-laden air, 20 paces in front of you, looms a veritable demon of enormous size. You blanch. It's true! THEY DO HAVE MONSTERS!

Above: *The pulling strength of the elephant is put to good use.*

Below: *'I'll just sip a quick gallon or two.' Elephants love taking a dip.*

Flesh and blood, it moves rapidly towards you. It is horrible to behold: as big as a house, coated in armour and glistening spikes, the head grotesquely sprouting a writhing snake like that of the fabled Gorgon, and with legs the size of the trunks of oak trees.

The demon bears down on the front rank, and in a babble of cries and the thud of weapons falling to the ground, the cohort (ye gods!) is split. Men tumble as the demon smashes through, followed closely by yelling Carthaginian foot soldiers slashing left and right with sword and spear. Though you don't realise it, you and your comrades have seen your first *elephant*.

Within minutes several dozen of these biggest of all land animals have routed the famous legions of Rome, and Hanni-

bal of Carthage can celebrate a great victory – he and his army, and his elephants, have won the battle of Trebia.

Elephants had been used in battle before Hannibal of Carthage employed them so brilliantly, but not by the Romans. In fact probably few Roman soldiers had even seen one, let alone knew how to fight it. At Trebia these gigantic animals, carrying armour to protect the few vulnerable parts of their bodies from spears and lances, broke through the formations of infantry (foot soldiers) like modern tanks. The cavalry (horse-mounted soldiers) to the rear was in a shambles for horses have an instinctive dislike of elephants. It was

'Don't you dare try anything on while my mum's around!' A baby African elephant sticks close to its mother's side. He can look forward to a long life – up to 70 years!

only later when the Romans captured some elephants and learned for themselves how to train them for warfare that they understood how to combat them. In future battles foot soldiers would be instructed to part their ranks when the elephants charged at them, and then, as the mighty beasts rushed through, use their swords to slash at the creatures' Achilles tendons (the gristly tendons at the backs of their ankles) in order to disable them.

Hannibal's march

Hannibal's famous journey across the Alps with a large army and 37 elephants began in spring 218 BC on the Spanish coast south of Alicante in the Costa Blanca. As a life-long enemy of the Roman Empire, he hoped to conquer Italy for the rival empire of Carthage. He moved up the coast and into France until he reached the River Rhone. To fool the Romans into thinking that he wasn't interested in crossing over the Alps into Italy, he then turned north up the left hand bank of the Rhone. Once the Romans had been fooled into thinking he was on a harmless expedition against the Gauls, he quickly turned eastwards

again, crossed the Rhone by rafts, and marched for the Alps. Amazingly, he crossed the high mountains, probably via the pass of Mont Genevre, without losing a single elephant to disease or injury. He descended into Italy and began a series of victorious battles by defeating the tribe that inhabited the city of Turin. The terrorising effect of the elephants on men who had never seen or heard of such creatures, together with their immense bulk and unstoppable power, gave Hannibal's army a formidable advantage.

In April 1988, I retraced the route of Hannibal's epic march in the company of Ian Botham, the English cricketer, and three Indian elephants from an Italian

circus, and we successfully raised a large amount of money for the Leukaemia Research Fund in the process. Our elephants fared as well as Hannibal's though we only asked them to walk a few miles each day at a speed they chose. The rest of the time they spent travelling by circus wagon to the next stop, where they were turned out into a field, to wait for us to catch up with them. My job was to act as Jumbo GP and walk with them to see that they stayed in tiptop condition. The elephants arrived in Turin fitter than me!

There used to be more than 350 different kinds of elephant on earth, but almost all became extinct long before Hannibal defeated the Roman army at Trebia. By

The most formidable of all land animals. An elephant herd on the march in Namibia.

then there were only the two species we know today – the *African* and the *Indian* (also known as the Asiatic) elephant. We don't know for sure which kind of elephant Hannibal used on his expedition. Some historians say African – Hannibal came from Carthage which was an ancient town in North Africa, in what today is Tunisia. Indeed, there are ancient Carthaginian coins of Hannibal's time which are engraved with unmistakable African elephants. One way you can recognise an African elephant is by its much larger ears. But there are other experts who think Indian elephants were used, as they are easier to train. There are Italian coins issued about the time Hannibal marched into Italy that bear the images of Indian elephants. This is a mystery that will probably never be solved.

Fearless and formidable

Elephants are naturally fearless and for- midable animals. Weighing up to 6 tonnes, eating 200-300 kg of food a day, and with thick, but sensitive skins, they have no natural enemies, although tigers may infrequently take them on. They are short-sighted, but possess marvellous hearing and a sharp sense of smell.

An ancient forerunner of the armoured car: war elephants were also used by Indian Rajahs.

> *Seest thou not*
> *How thy Lord dealt*
> *With the Companions*
> *Of the Elephant.*
> *Did He not make*
> *Their treacherous plan*
> *Go astray?*
> *And He sent against them*
> *Flights of birds*
> *Striking them with stones*
> *Of baked clay.*

This verse or Sura is called 'The Elephant'. It comes from the Holy Koran of Islam and refers to an historical event that happened about the year AD 570 when Mecca was invaded by the Christian Abraha of Abyssinia with his war elephants. The birds which flung stones at the invaders were thought to have caused an epidemic, characterised by sores and boils, that ravaged the Christians; this may be a reference to an outbreak of plague.

THE SUBMARINE SOLDIER

*I*magine. You are Lieutenant Yuri Zhukov of the Special Services Underwater Unit, Red Banner fleet, Russian Navy. The mission, like all others, is TOP SECRET. A new design of American frigate with a revolutionary propulsion system has been put into service according to intelligence reports received from the Soviet Embassy in Washington. The ship is faster and quieter by far than anything that the USSR possesses. What the spies *haven't* been able to discover, however, is what the new system looks like when fitted to a vessel. In place of a propeller there exists – what? Only one way to find out – go and take a look underwater.

And now one of the new frigates is on a visit to Portsmouth in southern England. The harbour is heavily guarded on land, and the vessel is surrounded by patrol boats that circle her protectively night and day. Your commander has given you your orders: 'Go in by silent nuclear submarine to a point about two miles off Gosport beach. Ride on an underwater scooter to the harbour mouth with an incoming tide. After that, Yuri, you must do it the hard way. Leave the scooter and swim in, 4 metres deep.'

The time is midnight on a moonless night. You are clad in an all-black wet suit with your face blackened. Strapped to your back are two air tanks painted black, part of a sophisticated breathing system that will not release tell-tale air bubbles to the surface once you are underwater. You will navigate by luminous instruments attached to your wrist. Shutting off the scooter's motor, you leave it lying as planned beneath an old iron buoy. With a powerful kick of your flippers, you glide into the cold darkness. Soon you see glimpses of light through the murky depths of the water, coming down from the harbour buildings and the moored ships. The water becomes dark-grey instead of black. You can pick out a ship's keel in the deep gloom. Checking your

Three 'Flippers' show their teeth. The teeth of bottle-nosed dolphins are not for chewing but rather grabbing hold of fish.

plastic map with a tiny water-proof pencil-torch, you change course. Another 200 metres maybe. There is the low chugging of a patrol boat overhead. You hang in the water till it passes. There – a black wall emerges out of the half-darkness; it is the frigate's hull. You look around you, turning in the water and listening intently – no sign of frogmen guarding the ship. You feel elated – no-one knows you are here, no-one would expect you. You are as black and silent as the deep water itself, invisible to their searchlights, undetected by their sonar. You move on, feeling for the mini-camera attached to your belt.

Suddenly you sense something near you and jerk your head to your right. A shape, a shadow is cutting through the water straight towards you! It travels too fast, too smoothly for a man. A shark? No – not in these waters. A second later the bayonet strapped to the head of a *dolphin* slams into your chest. With one last gasp you sink helplessly to the bottom, all consciousness draining away. The frigate's secret remains a secret. The dolphin sentry swims off with a leisurely upward

flick of his tail, for *his* sonar tells him that you were alone. For him the threat is over and his task accomplished.

Although the above story is horrific and may sound bit far-fetched, Atlantic bottle-nosed dolphins (the 'Flipper' you see on TV and in marinelands) really have been trained to do this sort of deadly guard duty, and have seen active service with the US armed forces for many years. In Vietnam, for example, their function was to guard harbours and ships at anchor against enemy frogmen; in Nicaragua they planted mines, and in the Arabian Gulf they searched for them.

For over 25 years the US Navy has maintained an Undersea Warfare Department to study the potential of the fighting dolphin. This has, incidentally, made many valuable scientific discoveries which have helped us to understand better this magical mammal and to unravel some of its secrets. Spin-off from the military dolphin programme has been of great benefit to research into human deafness and blindness, and into serious health threats that face deep-sea divers.

Living torpedo

Dolphins are highly-qualified recruits for modern sea warfare, I'm sad to say. They are intelligent, nimble, fast-moving creatures, with great strength and many inbuilt mechanisms for mastering the undersea world. They can be trained to fill various roles, particularly that of silent-running and elusive living torpedoes!

Though dolphins have large, efficient eyes which see well both above and underwater, it is their *sonar* ability which enables them to function just as well in pitch darkness, at night or far beneath the waves. The dolphin sends out a beam of sound 'blips' that bounce off distant objects, producing an echo that returns to the animal and which is analysed by it. These echoes are received, oddly, by the tip of the chin (*beak*) and the 'armpits' (where the flippers join the chest wall), and they are channelled by sound-conducting pathways to the well-developed internal ears. With its sonar system, a dolphin can *hear* the scene around it. The echoes tell the dolphin where, and exactly what, a far-away object is, and what it is doing. Dolphins can distinguish for example between a herring, a small shark and a mackerel. They can even tell the difference between different kinds of metal.

Although much of the US Navy's work with dolphins is still classified as secret, it seems probable that they possess animals which can identify particular types of sub-

Swimming at speed, dolphins often leap exuberantly out of the water. Two Pacific bottle-nosed dolphins enjoy the sunshine on their backs.

marines and other craft. Dolphins have been trained to carry magnetic limpet mines and stick them onto the hulls of enemy vessels. Their speed and manoeuvrability pose immense problems for defending frogmen and harbour security systems. So far nobody has developed the idea of having trained killer whales to act as watch dogs to combat dolphin raiders! Dolphins cut through the water at speeds of 40 kmh or more, their special skin eliminating drag and turbulence; and they can kill with a powerful blow of their

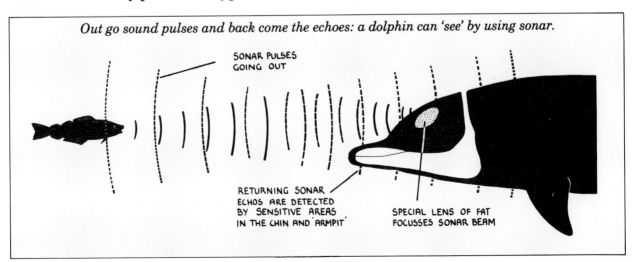

Out go sound pulses and back come the echoes: a dolphin can 'see' by using sonar.

SONAR PULSES GOING OUT

RETURNING SONAR ECHOS ARE DETECTED BY SENSITIVE AREAS IN THE CHIN AND 'ARMPIT'

SPECIAL LENS OF FAT FOCUSSES SONAR BEAM

closed jaws. They frequently kill marauding sharks that menace baby dolphins by punching them in the under-belly in this way. To avoid accidents, friendly Navy frogmen identify themselves to their sentry dolphins by wearing electronic 'bleepers' on their belts. These emit a sound signal that the dolphins have been trained to recognise. Nevertheless the US Navy has admitted that things have occasionally gone wrong and that the dolphins have mistakenly attacked and killed their own men.

Dolphins, and even sealions and small whales, have been trained in America to

The friendly and inquisitive bottle-nosed dolphin. What a pity it should sometimes be trained for military purposes.

locate mines and missiles underwater. Once found, the animal will swim down to the object carrying a device in its mouth which is attached to the object by means of a magnet or a spring-loaded clamp. A small compressed gas cylinder then automatically inflates a balloon which rises to the surface on a length of cable, so marking the object's position. Sometimes the balloons are big enough to lift the mine or missile up to waiting scientists.

A special relationship

Dolphins have many qualities that make them valued members of the Navy. They can dive deep and stay underwater for long periods of time. They can work easily without light in the dark depths of the sea. And once their job is done, they can rise rapidly again to the water's surface without getting the 'bends'; a dangerous condition caused by bubbles of nitrogen gas appearing in the blood. Of course the key to it all is that dolphins love to work with or for human beings. Long ago the Romans called in wild dolphins each year to help them herd fish into traps on the French coast near Marseille, rewarding them afterwards, it is said, with 'bread soaked in wine'; and we regularly hear of drowning people being saved by dolphins which have supported them and pushed them towards the shore.

What a tragedy that such wonderful creatures should ever have to be involved in man's dirty business of war and destruction.

Above: *A streamlined fast-moving species of the deep ocean, the Pacific white-sided dolphin.*

Below: *Making friends. This air-breathing mammal is quite happy to come out of the water and be stroked.*

105

AIRBORNE SECRET AGENTS

*I*magine. It is the end of November in the year 1870. You, Henriette Crapaud, sit in a cold, dark room near the cathedral of Nôtre Dame in Paris, France, wondering whether you can ever bring yourself to eat the piece of roasted rat that Mme Blanc, the concierge, has prepared for you. Rats, weeds, once even a dog – this is what hunger has brought you to. But you are not alone – all the citizens of Paris are starving, and disease is rife. There seems to be no end in sight. With Prussian armies besieging the capital and the air trembling with the boom of shell fire, there is despair everywhere. The Emperor Napoleon III has been captured and the statesman Gambetta has escaped from Paris by hot air balloon to try to raise an army to relieve the city, but like most folk you reckon it can only finish in a humiliating surrender to the Germans.

You are an assistant to the Parisian inventor and engineer M. Prudent Dagron, who nowadays earns barely a *sou* and cannot afford to pay your wages. But he's a good man, and maybe when the war is over he will take you to London to see some of the new English machines he talks about so much.

Unable to face the food, you put on your bonnet, coat and muffler, leave the house,

The sheer beauty of fantail pigeons rising into the air against a winter sun.

and walk across the Pont Sully. You pass a group of grimy soldiers huddled around a brazier, eating blackened onions. After five minutes you reach M. Dagron's workshop. As usual the inventor is seated at a bench littered with tools, glistening brass instruments and bottles of chemicals. A tall, bewhiskered man in a faded, blue, military uniform is standing by the window.

'Bonjour, Monsieur,' you say as you enter.

'Bonjour, Henriette,' replies Dagron. 'Oh, this is Captain de la Grange of the Imperial Artillery.' You shake hands with the stranger then go to your bench to begin your work.

'Henriette, Captain de la Grange has come to us with a problem – and I think we can help.'

'What is that, Monsieur?'

'The garrison here in Paris urgently needs to send maps of the disposition of our troops to the Commander-in-Chief with the French forces south of Versailles.'

The secret agent successfully carries the microfilm through the enemy lines.

You frown, puzzled. 'But how can we help, Monsieur?'

'The maps, my dear girl, are numerous and bulky – they must be photographed.'

M. Dagron has been a keen photographer for years – his workshop reeks of burnt magnesium flare powder. But you are still puzzled. 'But the photographs will also be big, Monsieur – what will you do with them?'

Dagron smiles. 'The Englishman, Henriette, the Englishman. He gave me the idea. Way back in 1853 when I first went to London, I met an Englishman, John Dancer, a maker of optical instruments who had recently reduced a full page of *The Times* newspaper to a dot barely 1.6 mm across! A sort of reduction photography! I have the lenses and the camera. I'll do the same.'

'M. Dagron here says he can shrink our maps to pinheads,' interrupts the Captain. 'A great idea!'

A pigeon, serving with the Army Pigeon Service in Africa in 1945 carries a special container on its back.

'And how will you send the photographed dots through the German lines, Monsieur?'

'Simple, Henriette, simple,' replies Dagron with a soft chuckle. 'Over their heads! By *pigeon*, my dear girl. A pigeon shall be our secret courier!'

Microdot carriers

It really happened that way. Prudent Dagron *did* photograph and reduce to the size of dots many pages of military information. He is recognised as the inventor of the 'microdot' which is still employed by spies and secret agents. The dots were printed onto photographic emulsion which was then wound into a thin tube and fastened to a pigeon's tail feathers. One pigeon could carry 18 emulsion films

108

and each film could contain up to 3,000 messages. The pigeons returned to their home lofts in the countryside outside Paris flying over the city's barricades. The film was recovered from the tube, and the dots were then magnified and read using a 'magic lantern' projector. And so the pigeon was enlisted into the French army's Intelligence Service.

Pigeons were first domesticated in Ancient Egypt around 3,000 BC and had been used as messengers long before M. Dagron thought of his microdots. The Sultan of Baghdad set up a pigeon-post system in the year 1150 AD. It lasted for 108 years until Baghdad fell to the Mongol invaders. And in France during the 1848 Revolution it was common for short messages to be sent on pieces of paper attached to pigeons for publication in French and Belgian newspapers.

During the twentieth-century the pigeon has played an important role in espionage. In the early 1900s, Herr Neubronner, a German, developed a miniature automatic camera weighing a mere 70 gm which could be carried aloft by pigeons to be used for spying and military reconnaissance. During the First World War (1914-18) the French Army employed thousands of pigeons to carry vital messages, and one bird which died after a successful mission flying through intense artillery fire at Verdun was actually awarded a posthumous Legion d'Honneur, the Republic's highest decoration. In the Second World War (1939-45) British planes dropped boxes of homing pigeons by parachute into German-occupied Europe to be used by the resistance fighters to fly messages to London.

The choice of pigeons to do such important work was quite natural. A common, domesticated species, the bird can reach speeds of 96 kmh and can cover distances of perhaps, as much as 12,800 km. An enemy wanting to intercept pigeon-borne letters might perhaps think of using birds of prey like falcons as 'fighters'. But first he would have the very difficult task of identifying pigeons 'on active service'.

Many experts, however, consider that no peregrine falcon in level flight could catch a fast racing pigeon, although these hawks can *dive* at 131 kmh.

A natural counter-spy, the peregrine falcon could be used to intercept message-carrying pigeons.

Amazing navigation

The master trick that the pigeon shares with many other birds, is its ability to find its way through the skies. Scientists still do not fully understand the pigeon's amazing ability to navigate with precision. They can do it by day or by night and with the sun, moon and stars behind cloud. It appears that they use a complicated system involving taking sitings of the sun or stars, perhaps by means of an organ in their eye called a pecten, much in the same way as a sailor uses a sextant. Some scientists believe the pecten also functions as a magnetic compass. Quantities of magnetic iron, which form a simple

Right lads, see you at the finishing line. Racing pigeons in their home loft.

compass, have been found in the skull of the pigeon, and it is known that pigeons can get lost if flying over places where large underground iron deposits distort the earth's normal magnetic field. Perhaps pigeons plot their courses by reference to our planet's invisible lines of magnetic force. This would account for the fact that pigeons can find their way home even on the cloudiest night when no stars are visible in the skies.

As well as the pecten and the compass, pigeons also possess an in-built biological

'clock' together with the ability to read the star map of the heavens and, when nearer home, to recognise familiar landmarks. Just as for a human navigator, a clock and a map will help the pigeon to judge how far it has travelled, and when it is time to change course.

Of all the military uses of animals, the one of which I most approve is the 'spy in the sky' role of the pigeon. These familiar birds of London's Trafalgar Square and Manhattan's concrete jungle must have saved many human lives.

Right: *The natural navigator. Birds like this pigeon possess an in-built clock, compass, star-map and possible sextant.*

Below: *Ultra-fast flash photography catches a pigeon about to land on its perch.*

ANIMALS THAT CHANGED HISTORY

Imagine. It is June in the Year of Our Lord 1099 in the land we now call Turkey, not far from the important city of Antioch. For you, Count Roland of Moze, these are stirring times. The First Crusade began two years ago when, blessed by the Pope and inspired by the fiery, wandering preacher, Peter the Hermit, 300,000 Christians, mainly Normans, knights and nobles, peasants and priests, merchants and mercenaries, set out from Europe with the Cross as their standard to recover the Holy City, Jerusalem, from the grip of the Seljuks, an Islamic Turkish tribe. You recall well the fierce fighting as you passed through the Byzantine kingdoms of Hungary and Bulgaria, the gathering of the hosts at Constantinople in Spring 1097 and the great cathedral of Santa Sophia packed with armoured men at High Mass. You remember too the first clashes with the Seljuks who rode into battle under the green banner of the Prophet Mohammed. And you will never forget the heat, the searing heat, of Asia Minor.

Now, in a column 5 km long, archers marching in front, plumed knights prancing behind, you ride on your faithful black stallion. The arid, grey land, broken only by low hillocks of crumbling rock, stretches in all directions to meet a grey sky on an imperceptible horizon. It is hot and humid. No wind, but many flies. Your chain-mail, helmet, leather under-jerkin, sword, axe and dagger weigh heavy. The stallion gleams with sweat where it is not covered in leather and mail. Oh, to fight again on the green swards of England or in the cool valleys of the Rhine! This ceaseless, sticky heat punishes more than any Mohammedan scimitar.

Still, once in the Holy Land, there will be riches to be had. Maybe you will be given a small kingdom for yourself by a grateful Pope. Yes, soon you will be in Jerusalem; there can be no doubt, for only a week ago the true Holy Lance that pierced the side of Our Saviour when He was on the cross was discovered – a sign of heaven's benediction indeed.

Your thoughts are rudely interrupted by a 'thwack' sound. An archer walking immediately in front of your horse falls to the ground, an arrow sprouting from his neck. Uproar breaks out at once. There is shouting and the metallic hiss of swords being unsheathed. Archers unshoulder their bows, horses snort and rear. Over to your right, 50 paces off, you see a horseman in turban and flowing robe disappearing behind a hillock. Mohammedans!

112

Horses as well as men suffered at the Battle of Waterloo.

Two of your armoured knights are already riding after him. They quickly return. 'Gone, my Lord,' one calls. No wonder, you think. These heathen bowmen on their light and agile horses carry no armour, and have often little more than rags to cover them. Norman knights clank around in iron on lumbering heavy steeds. By Our Lady, if only these Mohammedans would fight like we do in Europe. Steel against steel. But no! They prefer to harry us, pick us off piecemeal, all by dint of speed, surprise and flexibility. It's just not Christian!

So it was that crusader and Moslem *horses* met in battle, with large numbers of animals dying as a result, though in some encounters such as that at Jaffa in 1191, only two crusaders lost their lives. In all the most crucial battles and expeditions throughout history, the horse was present and played a leading role – in the conquests of Alexander the Great, at the Battle of Hastings in 1066, in the struggles between Royalists and Roundheads in the English Civil War, at the Battle of Waterloo in 1815, and in the American Civil War (1861-65), man and horse fought and died together. The names of individual battle horses have come down to us through the pages of our history books – there is *Bucephalus* who belonged to Alexander the Great, the only person who could mount him; *Incitatus*, the Roman Emperor Caligula's stallion that was said to have drunk wine out of a golden bucket; *White Surrey*, the favourite horse of King Richard III; and *Copenhagen*, the Duke of Wellington's faithful charger.

Ancestors of the horse

How did the horse develop to become man's most important domesticated animal? The story begins about 55 million years ago. Then the continents of Europe and North America were joined together in one land-mass. Here a little dog-like animal moved through the forests, browsing on low shrubs. This was *Hyracotherium*, ancestor of the horses and also of the rhinoceroses and tapirs. It was descended itself from forebears which had possessed the basic five toes per foot, and it had already lost two outer toes on its hind feet and one inner toe on its fore feet. The remaining toes looked dog-like, with pads; but as yet there was no sign of hooves. It had a short muzzle and a long tail held curved like a cat's.

As the ages passed, the descendants of Hyracotherium split off into numerous branches of the family tree. The rhinos and tapirs went their way and the horses went theirs. In the equine branch, many developments took place over thousands, even millions of years. Gradually more toes were discarded till finally a single, highly modified toe remained on each foot. The animal grew larger, developed teeth that were ideal for cropping and grinding grass, and acquired large, efficient eyes.

By about one million years ago, all the surviving equine descendants of Hyracotherium had settled into four main groups: the *horses*, the *asses*, the *half-*

An unlikely animal for the Grand National! Hyracotherium, the early ancestor of horses and ponies.

asses and the *zebras*. They were distributed in fairly specific areas of Africa, Europe and the Middle East, with almost no overlapping of the various groups. The zebras were to be found only in the south of Africa and the half-asses (ancestors of the *onager, kulan, kiang and dziggetai*, and of the *hemione* which became extinct about 100 years ago) were all from Asia. The asses, from which *donkeys* were developed, were purely from the north of Africa, and the horses (including *ponies*, which are simply horses under 14.2 hands high) were inhabitants of Europe and western Asia.

By the Ice Age, scientists can identify four major types of horse or pony existing in the world, and with the disappearance of all horses in the Americas by about 6,000 BC (why, we do not know), they were confined to Europe and western Asia. From those four types the cavalry horses of history as well as our modern horse and pony breeds are all descended.

Domestication of the horse began around 3,000 BC, almost certainly in eastern Europe and the steppes of western Asia (at about the same time the Sumerians started domesticating onagers in what is now Iraq). From these areas the domestic equine spread outwards after 2,000 BC, with the first animals being

tamed for riding and pack work, probably by reindeer herdsmen. Later they were broken for harnessing to chariots. Before 600 BC, all the 'horses' ridden or driven by ancient civilisations were in fact ponies!

This beautiful Arabian colt shows the fine quality inherited from the steeds of the Mohammaden horsemen.

Our ancestors looked at the horse with its strength and mobility and slowly began to realise how this fine beast could change things – not least in the art of warfare. At first the fighting men of Europe were foot soldiers; early Greek and Roman armies were composed almost solely of infantry, with sometimes just a sprinkling of mounted bow-men. The reason was that in the countries to the south and west of the Danube and Rhine Rivers, there existed as yet no breeds of horse suitable for military purposes. Besides, most of Greece was hilly, not the sort of country where cavalry could excel. In Asia however, where there was an abundance of flat land, the horse-soldiers predominated.

In London, the days of old are recalled by the ceremonial cavalry parade by the Queen's guard.

The cavalry are coming!

In the fifth century BC, when the Asiatic horsemen first came into contact with European foot soldiers, the idea of a combined army, with cavalry and infantry supporting one another, began to take root. Philip of Macedon, the great Greek king and general, founded the use of cavalry in the West. He created superb forces of horsemen, one cavalry-man to every six foot soldiers, and divided them into three sorts: the heavy armoured cavalry were for charging the enemy; the light cavalry (Hussars) acted as scouts and patrols; and the Dragoons were trained to fight on foot or on horseback. To defend his infantry against opposing cavalry, he massed the foot-soldiers into tight formations (phalanxes) armed with pikes 6 m long, to form an impenetrable hedge of steel. Philip's son, Alexander the Great, proved the effectiveness of this strategy in countless battles.

The Romans were rather slow in appreciating the value of cavalry, and when they eventually began to use horsemen in large numbers they made the serious mistake of separating them from the infantry. This error was the main cause of the decline of Rome's military power, for unsupported Roman cavalry were no match for the fierce barbarian horsemen who came riding in from the East, combining superb horsemanship with the added advantage of a highly-developed stirrup they had perfected, which meant they could mount their steed more easily, and gave them greater stability once on horseback.

At the end of the fourth century AD, cavalry became the main fighting force of

This fifteenth century war horse was as elegantly armoured as the knight who rode him.

European armies and remained so for over a thousand years. Between AD 500 and AD 1200 there were many well-equipped cavalry armies in the Middle East. In the West however, the key importance of the cavalry/infantry combination was forgotten. By the Middle Ages, Europe's preferred style of mounted fighting man was the knight, a self-contained 'armadillo' dependent on his heavy armour for safety and success, who wrongly assumed that he would always be opposed by a similarly iron-clad enemy. Heavy armour on a mounted man certainly gave him protection but it sacrificed his mobility, and the armour his horse now wore made matters even worse. By the mid-1300s some knights were so heavily armoured that, exhausted after repeated charges, their adversaries were able to roll them out of their saddles by grabbing their shoulders.

Haflinger ponies grazing on a Tyrollean meadow resemble the mounts of the Mongul horsemen.

Meanwhile the Mongols of the East, under the leadership of Genghis Khan, were showing what a disciplined, unarmoured cavalry could achieve. His men rode tough Mongolian ponies. Commanded in battle by means of signals from black or white flags during the day and coloured lanterns and whistling arrows at night, using smoke screens and fighting with bows and arrows to avoid close combat, they moved with impressive fluidity and flexibility – totally unlike their European counterparts. In the fifteenth century, Tamburlaine (Timur the lame), a chieftain from central Asia, repeated the empire-building success that Genghis Khan had achieved over 200 years before, but on horses that were bigger (cobs about 15.2 hands high) and of even better quality.

The fifteenth century saw the dawn of the age of gun-powder. As armour was not invulnerable to the bullet, it grew lighter, and the horse now carried a man armed with a hand cannon or arquebus.

When Cortes, the Spanish conquistador, invaded the Aztec kingdom on horseback in Mexico in 1519, his expedition almost failed; it was the horse that saved the day. The Aztecs had never before seen horses, and the animals tipped the balance in favour of the invaders, often by scaring the natives into fleeing. But for the horse, the later history of South America would have taken a totally different course, and Spanish would not now be the language of countries from Mexico to Argentina.

As the centuries passed cavalry squadrons played major roles in the Napoleonic wars, the Boer War in South Africa and the First World War. A mere 50 years ago mounted soldiers were invaluable in the rough, mountainous terrain of Spain during the Civil War. In the Second World War however, the war-horse was increasingly replaced by a new kind of iron horse, the tank and the armoured car, though the horse's cousin, the mule, played a vital role in carrying heavy loads, including weapons and ammunition through many rugged places. In the Burmese jungle where allied troops fought the Japanese, mules were used to negotiate narrow, steep tracks. In order to prevent them alerting the enemy by uttering their characteristic braying sounds, army veterinary surgeons were called upon to operate on their larynxes (voice-boxes)

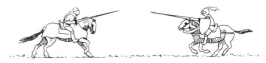

Right: *August 1917. Pack mules carry shells through the appalling mud of the battlefield.*

Below: *The American Indians had never seen a horse before.*

under anaesthetic in order to quieten their vocal cords – regrettable but essential surgery under the circumstances.

The veterinary service

Army horses have for centuries had army veterinary surgeons to look after their health problems in the same way that army doctors attend to the troops. Before qualified vets did this work, army farriers (blacksmiths) tended sick and wounded

animals, and in the English army of the late sixteenth century military orders urged that there should always be 'a skillful Ferrar' who could judge soundness and lameness in the horses. In 1796 the British Army set up its Army Veterinary Service. Since then its vets have had not just horses as patients, but also camels, bullocks, cattle and donkeys. Most of the army vets' work then, as later, was in treating disease rather than battle wounds. In the Boer War one veterinary officer reported that of 4,170 cases of sickness in horses in his unit in two-and-a-half years of war, only 163 were due to bullet wounds and three to shell fire.

At the start of the First World War there were 53,000 horses in the British Army; there were six 250-'bed' (stall) veterinary hospitals, and 11 mobile veterinary units. As the war progressed however the number of horses rose to 450,000 with 18 2,000-'bed' veterinary hospitals! One curious consequence of the use of poison gas in that war was the issue of large gas masks to the horses. In the event, tens of thousands of horses were

In the First World War many horses wounded during battles were tended by the Army Veterinary Surgeons.

killed and wounded by gunshot wounds and bombs, but relatively few died from the effects of gas. In recognition of the Army Veterinary Corps' great work with horses during the war, King George V conferred the title 'Royal' upon it in 1918 and it became what it is known as today, the Royal Army Veterinary Corps.

In the Second World War, the RAVC accompanied pack animal units in Greece, Sicily, Italy, the Middle East, India and Burma. After this war they served again in Malaya, Kenya and Cyprus. As late as 1958 donkeys were employed to carry loads on the high mountain plateaux of Oman where the British Army was carrying out operations. One can imagine, in these days of guerilla warfare and civil unrest in Third World countries with difficult terrain, that horses, mules and donkeys, and their veterinarians, might well be called upon to serve with soldiers once more.

THE MODERN ARMY ANIMAL

It is 1962 in the battle-scarred area of Vietnam that the Americans call 'The Iron Triangle'. You, Ho-Chek, not long ago a peasant girl living in a village near Hanoi, sit cleaning your Kalashnikov rifle by the faint light of a lamp that is no more than a scrap of string in a tin cup full of old engine oil. Your chamber is a recess in the wall of a passageway barely big enough to hold three crouching people. The walls and roof are hard, dark soil and the air within is foul and humid. The passageway runs for 100 m east and west, and is connected by hidden trap doors to the main tunnel complex below. Down there, there are much bigger rooms, a small hospital, a kitchen, and several caches of explosives.

Sunlight, the green land, and the fresh, fragrant air are just 4 m above your head. But up there too is danger, destruction, and death. Napalm bombs, helicopter gunships and flame throwers brought by the armies of the United States, sear the once beautiful countryside with its tranquil paddy fields, vivid sunsets, lush jungle, water buffalo, and thatched hamlets. But still the Americans cannot believe, cannot know, with what effort and ingenuity you and your thousands of comrades in the Viet Cong have laboured to construct this vast underground labyrinth, this army camp in the earth, living like human moles. When they have sent men into the tunnels to investigate, they have encountered spiked traps, tethered poisonous snakes and trip-wired grenades; amongst all these dangers they have overlooked the concealed doorways and false walls.

By day you stay, fox-like, in the earth, but at night you emerge from the tunnels and go, clothed in black, shrouded by darkness, to attack and harass the enemy invader in his encampments.

'Ho-Chek.' Someone speaks your name softly. You raise the lamp and see the head of your section leader, Vam, emerging from the darkness in the western stretch of tunnel. He curls himself up against the wall of your chamber.

'We go soon?' you ask.

'Yes, Comrade.' He looks at his watch. 'In ten minutes. You know what you have to do?'

'Of course. Cut the wire exactly opposite the first parked helicopter. Wait for Comrade Ngi's diversion attack to begin in the north, and then go through with the explosives to position A.'

Vam nods.

'What though if the Americans do what they did last week?' you ask, trying not to

A dog training unit of the US army in the Second World War.

121

One of the most popular working dogs for the armed services and police – the German shepherd dog.

sound too apprehensive. 'Everything went well until their guard patrol discovered Comrade Pak and his unit, even though they were well concealed.'

'Pak died honourably,' replies Vam. 'They all did. But what you say is true, the Americans can find us, using those . . . those devils. But I have the answer here.

Hanoi command came up with the idea.' He pulls a small bag out of his tunic and hands it to you. 'Here. Take these and rub them all over you before we go. That will put them off.'

You open the bag and look at the contents – several rotting cloves of garlic and a few blackened onions. The smell is pungent. A smile, a rare sight these days, begins to form on your lips. Of course! This should take care of those accursed Yankee war *dogs*!

During the Vietnam War the Viet Cong guerillas found that the trained dogs, *German shepherds* and *Dobermann pinschers* mainly, employed by the US Army to guard bases and accompany patrols, could be countered at least as far as their important sense of smell was concerned, by rubbing one's body with, and wearing bags containing, very pongy things.

An order issued by the Viet Cong Military Command reads: 'To make the dogs lose their sense of direction when they are chasing us, confuse their sense of smell with mixed odours. Garlic, onions, perfumes like eau-de-Cologne and overripe peppercorns will all make difficulties for them. When we camouflage ourselves, we should use these items by spreading them either on our bodies or over the vent holes of our underground hideouts. When in close combat, aromatic foods like fried fish and roasted meat can be thrown to the dog to put him off. You should also discard your sweating jacket or shirt to distract him . . . '.

Nowadays armed forces of many nations enlist trained dogs to perform a variety of duties. They can guard, track, carry messages, act as attackers and defenders. The military make use of their superb senses of smell and hearing as well as their speed, strength, intelligence . . . and their sharp teeth!

Selected breeding

The dog evolved as a versatile hunting carnivore, full of stamina and able to cope with a range of environments. The wild canid family from which the domestic dog is descended are masters of the long distance chase, wearing down their prey by sheer persistence, quite unlike the brilliant, ultra-fast, but essentially short-distance, wild cats. Domestication of the dog began around 10,000 years ago; much later selected breeding gave us the multitude of breeds that we know today. Man shaped the breeding of dogs to his own requirements, thereby obtaining general working dogs, dogs with more specialised working skills, and decorative dogs. He ended up with dachshunds for badger hunting, collies to herd sheep and miniature poodles just to look pretty.

One of the duties of a modern fighting dog is to guard airfields.

Dogs were probably used as guards soon after they were first domesticated by primitive man. Social animals, loving to be part of a family, canine or human, they are quick to raise the alarm by barking when a stranger intrudes. The dog became the first, and is today the most important, of man's military animals.

In 2100 BC, King Hammurabi of Babylon sent his warriors into battle accompanied by huge, fierce hounds. In Ancient Rome *mastiffs* in light armour, carrying spikes and cauldrons of flaming sulphur and resin on their backs, would dash among the enemy soldiers causing havoc. These canine 'tough guys' were formed into platoons and placed with the legionaries on the front rank. British 'broad-mouthed' dogs were prized by the Romans for their pugnacity in war and also for combat in the games held in the amphitheatres of the Empire. In the Middle Ages, armoured dogs, fully clad in metal, were used particularly against mounted knights. King Henry VIII sent several

'Cave Canem!' I suppose mastiffs in the Roman armies must have understood commands in Latin.

This French army dog carried grenades to the frontline troops during the First World War.

hundred war dogs to Emperor Charles V of Spain to help him in his war with France, and they proved a great success. In the eighteenth century Frederick the Great used dogs both as sentries and as ammunition carriers when at war.

Training schools

At the beginning of the First World War, Britain had no official war dogs, though the Germans had over 6,000 ready and waiting. This was only remedied in 1916 when the first British war dog training school was established. Dogs were used at first as messengers, as guards, to locate wounded men (German war dogs were credited with saving at least 4,000 soldiers), and to a lesser extent, on patrols. *Airedales* and *collies* were at first the two

125

The boxer made a good guard for army posts in the Middle East during the First World War.

most popular breeds for the army, but eventually the Alsatian (German shepherd), a versatile, strong and intelligent animal, supplanted them. For tracking and mine detection work, *labradors* were to prove superb, and *boxers* were highly regarded as guards in Middle Eastern war zones.

In the Second World War dogs played a much bigger role than formerly, and sometimes in very unpleasant ways. They were trained by the Russians to carry out suicide missions against German tanks. They would run between the tracks of the vehicles with mines strapped to their backs. The mine would explode as soon as a vertical antennae attached to it touched the metal of the tank. I am glad to say that no-one trains dogs as 'living bombs' anymore!

In the British Army patrol dogs accompanied groups of soldiers on reconnaissance and, working silently, located by smell any hidden enemy. Then, like a gundog, they would freeze and 'point' in the manner of a setter or pointer. Mine-detecting dogs, again working by scent, could easily locate buried mines, either planted recently or long ago, at depths up to 30 cm. Dogs are better at this than most electronic sniffing devices! Some dogs were parachuted in with SAS units or the stretcher bearers of airborne divisions. These dogs were trained to search only for men lying in a prone, and therefore prob-

ably injured, position and to ignore all others. Such brave and clever dogs saved many allied soldiers' lives. Message-carrying dogs were trained to carry notes in a pouch on their collar between command posts and outposts or patrols.

Dogs continue to be trained and cared for by the British and other Armed Forces and have been on duty in Malaya, Kenya, Korea, Cyprus and, more recently, the Falklands and Northern Ireland. In Northern Ireland their abilities as guards and explosive-detectors have proved invaluable. The prestige and popularity of the fighting army dog has never been greater than at present. While army horses are nowadays only used for ceremonial purposes, the army dogs 'soldier on', and my colleagues the veterinarians of the RAVC and US Armed Forces have become specialists in canine medicine and surgery – 'horse-doctors' no longer.

The natural skills of a pointer accustomed to finding gamebirds, proved useful in the Second World War for locating injured soldiers.

Cry 'Havoc!' and let slip the dogs of war
Shakespeare *Julius Caesar* (Act III, Sc. i)

DESERT FIGHTERS

*I*magine. It is July 1950 in the north-eastern desert of Arabia, and you, Salim bin Ahmed of the Bani Hajir tribe, crouch pressed up against the *camel*'s flank, your *abba* (cloak) pulled over your head. The animal is kneeling with its tailend turned to the howling wind. Stinging sand drives with the wind turning the air the colour of lentil broth, and you cannot see the rest of the herd that should be lying but a few metres off. By the beard of the Prophet, this storm is insufferable! The summer heat alone is bad enough, but the flying sand makes breathing almost impossible.

The sandstorm began about three hours ago as a small black cloud on the horizon that grew quickly and spread to claim the whole border between sky and desert.

Then it clawed its way up the heavens to blot out the sun. *Wallah!* Let it not be true, as the Kuwaiti bedou say, that such storms will last for three, seven or even 14 days! Your father, camped at the wells half a day's camel-ride away will be worried. This is the first time he has trusted you to take his camels to the grazing on your own. Still, all will be well, you have two skins full of water.

Another hour passes miserably and you reach under your *dish-dasha* (smock) for the bag of dates your mother gave you. The sand has even got to them and coated them in grit. Just then the unthinkable happens. Out of the swirling brown cloud

To me one of the most romantic scenes in the world; camels at home in the deep desert.

Steady under gunfire, a camel served as a multi-purpose fighting vehicle in the desert long before Landrovers and armoured cars were invented.

several dark shapes loom. Camels and riders! Who . . . ?

'*Al-guwa!*' a gruff voice calls the greeting. 'What have we here?' Six bedou riders carrying rifles move up to you.

'A young lad of the Bani Hajir far away from his mother, eh?' Raiders from the Ajman tribe to the north!

'I am Salim bin Ahmed' you shout above the storm, throwing a quick glance at your rifle in its cloth holster half-covered by the camel. No use, the raiders already have their guns pointing at you. One of the strangers taps your camel with his stick and it rises making a grumbling gurgle. He snatches its headrope.

'Well, Salim bin Ahmed, we are going to lift your camels. You should thank Allah we did not shoot you.'

Burning with anger, unable to do anything to save your family's camels from these arrogant robbers, you spit in the sand. 'My father and the Bani Hajir will

descend upon you like vultures on dead goats,' you say through gritted teeth. 'You will regret this day!'

The Ajmanis laugh behind the *kaffiyas* pulled across their faces against the sand. Their leader raises his rifle and fires one shot into the air. 'Brave words, my little gazelle, but it is your good fortune we take your camels and not your life.' He pulls on his camel's head-rope to turn it and the others do likewise.

'*Yaum-kum sa'id*' they shout as they disappear into the storm. It means literally 'Have a happy day!'. May the *djinns* (spirits) of the sandstorm whirl them away.

For thousands of years camels were ideal for military purposes in desert areas. The bedou nomads of Arabia used them until quite recently for raids like the one described above, and for more serious acts of warfare. Traditionally one of the great

'sports' of the bedou was raiding. Such forays rarely lead to much bloodshed and were conducted according to a gentlemanly rule book which insisted that women be unharmed and included a list of 'permitted' items, including goats, camels, carpets and coffee pots, which could be 'legitimately' snatched. A favourite raiding time was summer when camels graze far from the wells, and under the cover of sandstorms. Raiders sometimes travelled great distances of 250 miles or more to attack a target, and for such gruelling desert journeys the camel was their vehicle. In raids of up to 100 miles distance a mixture of camels and horses in equal numbers was usually employed.

A camel can carry heavy loads for long distances without feeding or drinking.

The ungainly-looking leg of the camel is perfect for desert travel.

The ship of the desert

The camel, familiarly called 'the ship of the desert', is well designed for a military role that only since the Second World War has been taken over fully by tracked mechanical vehicles, armoured cars and helicopters. Just look at a camel's capabilities! It carries concentrated rations in the form of special fat in a 'rucksack', the hump, on its back, enabling it to go for many days without food. Unlike most other mammals it can lose one-third of its body weight in the form of water without becoming ill. The blood stays thin to a point at which it would have thickened fatally in a dog or horse. Apart from its resistance to water loss, the camel saves every drop of the precious liquid that it can by not panting, and by concentrating its urine and by only passing small quantities, taking the waste products back into its body for conversion into food. Thus it conserves water and allows its body to 'dry out' to a degree that would prove rapidly fatal for a human being. Camels have been known to go for three weeks without water. When they are at last able

BUUURP! The camel is a frequent grumbler and gurgler.

to drink their fill, they can regain 30 per cent of their weight in just ten minutes.

Other design features of the camel which assist a desert lifestyle are an insulating coat of thick hair which keeps heat *out* during the day, and conserves body heat during the often freezing desert nights; round, flat feet, that are good for spreading the weight when walking on soft sand; long, lush eyelashes which keep sand out of the eyes when the lids are half-closed but still permit vision; and slot-like closeable nostrils, which also act as a protection against blowing sand.

The British Army used camels in many campaigns in the Middle East. Camels are in their prime at about nine years of age and the Army considered seven to 12 year olds as being suitable for military purposes. There are different breeds of camel with some better adapted to certain conditions than others. Those from the fertile Egyptian delta are not as able to withstand periods of drought and scarce

food as desert-bred animals. Breeds from the Central Asian steppes are small and shaggy with manes like lions; they work well in deep snow but cannot stand the desert heat. Indian camels survive heat and thirst well, as do the strong, compact and short-legged Ethiopian camels. Somalian camels are lightly built, can go for long periods without water, but aren't as strong as the Indian ones.

Stoicism and stamina

Good camels have amazing stamina. They can carry 120-220 kg for 32 km a day. After a battle near Basra, Iraq, in 1915, a messenger rode one 848 km in five and a half days to bring news to the Saudi king of a British victory over the Turks. The animals can travel for up to 160 km with rest halts every 32 km or so at a fast pace of 16 kmh. For short distances they can manage 21 kmh.

Camels are less liable to panic under gunfire than other animals and if made to kneel will remain so, quiet and contented. Some breeds such as the Somali, are rather nervous of strangers and are also

more jumpy at night. They bear pain with great fortitude and, unfortunately, will continue to work beyond a point of exhaustion at which other species would give up or collapse. They cannot jump across ditches – gaps in the ground over which they cannot stride constitute major obstacles; but they are strong swimmers and have been seen crossing the Nile even where the river is at its broadest and the current powerful.

The first Camel Corps to serve with the British Army was formed in 1884 in Egypt as part of a relief expedition going to Khartoum to rescue General Gordon. Later the Corps became a permanent part

The glamorous Camel Corps served efficiently in desert campaigns.

of the Army in Egypt and saw active service there, in Somalia, Palestine and other places.

One of the most romantic modern figures to be associated with battle camels was the Englishman T.E. Lawrence (Lawrence of Arabia) who fought with the Arabs against the Turks between 1915 and 1919. A brilliant leader of guerillas mounted both on camels and horses, he was particularly successful at wrecking Turkish trains, to such an extent that a large reward was offered for the capture of 'El Orens, destroyer of engines'!

> *Death is a black camel, which kneels at the gates of all.*
> Abd-El-Kader

These Toureg nomads carried out raids on their camels until fairly recently.

If you ever get the chance to ride a camel, perhaps when on holiday or at the zoo, take it. The animal's gait is quite different from that of a horse or pony and takes a little getting used to. I find it very exciting. The sight of Bedou nomads riding camels in the deep desert (they are still to be found in countries bordering the Arabian Gulf) is one of the most stirring and romantic things that I can recall. Bedou raiders of the Ajmani tribe would ride on a camel sitting *behind* the hump on a straw-stuffed mattress attached by ropes on the left and right, fixed to a girth in front of the hump. Other Bedou prefer to sit on the hump itself, a sheepskin saddle beneath them, with a pointed wooden pommel rising in front and another behind.

133

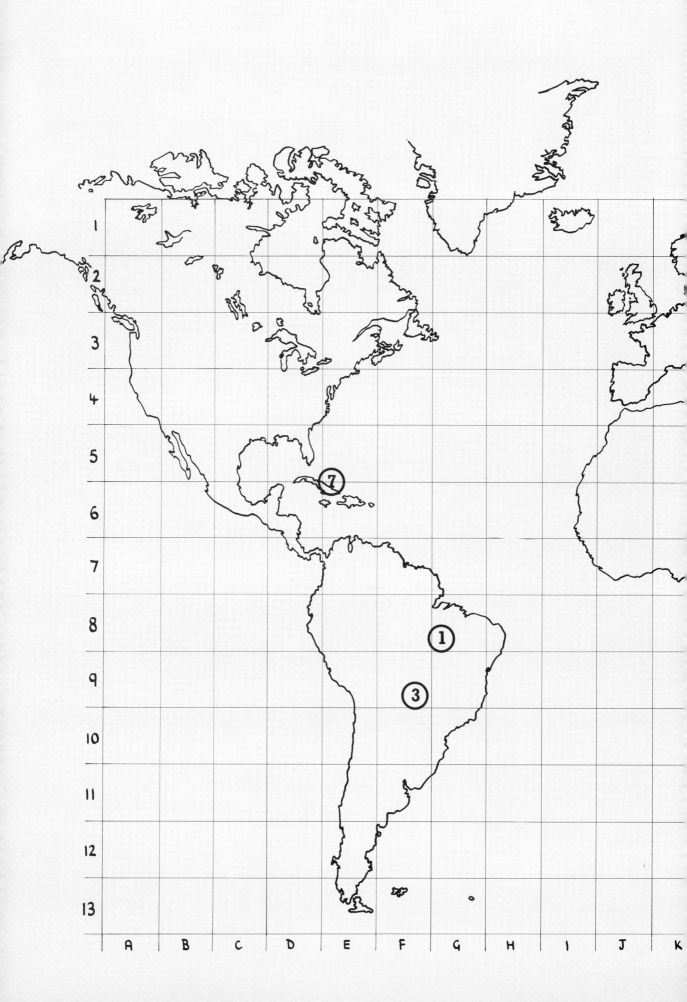

ANIMALS

IN

DANGER

② 2

④ 4

⑤ 5

⑥ 6

⑧ 8

⑨ 9

L M N O P Q R S T U V

Operation Minerva

TOP SECRET

Read, memorise and then destroy this document.

The location of the headquarters of The Organisation is known to only a few people. On the door as you arrive for briefing, you see the brass plate and its inscriptions in large letters:

CIA
(Campaign against Insensitivity towards Animals)

KGB
(Keen Guardian Biologists)

MI5
(Mammal Intelligence Unit 5)

After electronic screening, you are admitted to my office. The following conversation is recorded by my monitors:

'Good morning, my code name is **D**. Sit down, please, and let me outline the mission ahead of you.

'Conservation of wildlife, the protection of endangered species – all of us are familiar with, and whole-heartedly approve of, the idea. Every day we read in the newspapers of some threat – natural disasters or aspects of human activity – that are claiming the lives of some animal or plant that has survived on this planet for millions of years, but is now in imminent danger of vanishing for ever. Pandas starving when the bamboo flowers once in a hundred years, whales still hunted by the Japanese and Icelanders, rainforests burned deliberately to provide more space for cattle ranching, oil slicks and pesticides poisoning shellfish, sea birds and sea otters.

'Changes in the way man uses the world that he shares with other living creatures threaten not only famous species like rhinos and giant otters, but also many lesser known but equally fascinating animals that have their rightful place in the scheme of things – lizards, spiders, the minute creatures that make coral, and all sorts of rare insect.

'I have decided to enlist you in my elite intelligence service as an undercover agent. Your code name for the operation is Treble Zero, **000**. Your mission is to investigate and report on status, whereabouts, enemies of, ten "target" animals. They were last seen in different parts of the world. All are in danger, all need our help. You must set out, locate and assess the situation for each of the ten and then report back here to mission control. Your equipment – a map with grid references is provided at the beginning of this book – otherwise you must rely on your wits and physical fitness. Communicate on secure satellite channel 22. And leave your Biretta automatic behind!

'The risks: you are up against formidable opposition, the selfish human being in his many guises – governments, industrialists, criminals, the unthinking man in the street, often uninformed and frequently a source of pollution.

'Here are your dossiers containing key information on the targets. The operation is code-named "Minerva" after the Roman Goddess of Wisdom, whose symbol was the owl. The password – **"Owl-Hoot"**.

'Good luck and good hunting, **000**!'

Degree of survival threat for each target is colour-coded as follows:

Red: Endangered and may soon be extinct in the wild.

Orange: Endangered and may soon be extinct in the wild. Some populations flourishing in captivity.

Yellow: At risk with numbers of animals falling rapidly.

Green: Some threat but not at present in danger of extinction.

OPERATION MINERVA:

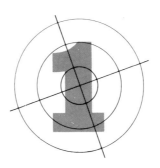

NAME ☐ Giant Otter

ALIAS ☐ *Pteronura brasiliensis*

REPORTED SEEN ☐ Map ref G8

BACKGROUND ☐ This beautiful animal can grow to a length of almost 2 m from nose to tail tip and weigh as much as 35 kg. It is the biggest, and probably the rarest, of all otters with a most handsome velvety, chocolate-brown coat that sports creamy white patches or streaks on the underparts, particularly the throat area. As a result the *giant otter* frequently looks as if he were wearing a white tie, cravat or necklace to accompany a smart brown suit; hence one of its local names is 'Lobo corbata' – which means 'wolf with a tie'!

Other locations where it can be seen ☐
Zoos at MADRID (Spain), DUISBURG (Germany).

Estimated degree of survival threat ☐
Condition orange. Numbers declining over most of its range.

Field report from 000 to D.
Operation Minerva. Top priority.
24 August. 06.00 hrs.
Have located the giant otter. Once the species was to be found over most of the north-eastern and central areas of South America, but in many places it has completely disappeared or been reduced to small scattered populations, sometimes numbering 20, but more usually less.
Details ☐ Otters are amphibious carnivores belonging to the weasel family of mammals which also includes skunks,

The giant otter of South America is a master swimmer.

mink and badgers. There are 12 species of otter living in various parts of the world. Only one species is wholly marine, seldom coming ashore – the delightful *sea otter* which loves to float on its back in the water, cracking shellfish on its chest with its nimble forepaws. The others mess about mainly or exclusively in freshwater rivers, lakes and streams.

Otters are intelligent, inquisitive, playful, hyper-active animals. They are brilliant swimmers, being equipped with a streamlined body, tightly packed waterproof body hair, webbed feet in most species, including the giant, and a strong rudder-like tail which is somewhat flattened. They feed on water-living creatures which they find by using their eyes, touch and vibration-responsive whiskers and, in those otters which do not have claws, sensitive 'finger' tips. Even the smaller kinds of otter have a powerful

A seafood lunch in the sunny Pacific – a sea otter munches abalone.

bite and I have seen terrible wounds inflicted on humans who took liberties with them.

Giant otters chase fish under water and also catch crabs. They hunt mainly by day, and after catching their prey with their mouths, hold it in their forepaws and eat its head first, often while lounging in shallow water. They live in slow-running rivers, creeks, lakes and marshes in forested areas. When the rivers flood the forest during the rainy season, the fish go with the flood water to spawn and the otters follow.

These beautiful creatures form strong pair-bonds, with the female usually being the boss! They are territorial animals, marking their property with droppings (spraints) and urine left at specific places which they clear of vegetation to make a

The endangered giant otter has caught his dinner.

A pair of giant otters bask on a log beside the Amazon.

flat half-circle. They 'garden' the marked areas regularly to keep them tidy and free from overgrowth of plants. Giant otter groups have communal lavatories where urine and droppings are mixed with the soil or mud by thorough kneading with the front and hind paws.

Giant otters can be quite noisy. They have a wide repertoire of sounds which they can use for communication, and I have heard humming noises, whistles, squeals, coos, growls and barks.

Litters of one to five, but usually two, cubs are born in a holt (den) burrowed into a river bank, after a pregnancy of 65-70 days. Giant otters can live for about 12 years in the wild and much longer in zoos. *Message ends.*

D to 000. How many giant otters do you estimate still exist?

000 to D. Numbers unknown, but undoubtedly falling rapidly.

D to 000. Please identify enemies of giant otter.

000 to D. Re. Giant otter enemies.

1. Man. Hunting the otter to provide pelts for the fur trade was, and still remains, a major threat. Approximately 2,000 skins a year were at one time being exported from Brazil alone. Although hunting bans were introduced in the 1970s, much illegal poaching continues. Once again the fur trade has a lot to answer for.

2. Man. Destruction of forests for timber and to exploit land for agriculture and mining, as well as the draining of vast areas, has severely affected the availability of the shallow creeks and seasonal flooding that are so important to the giant otter lifestyle.

3. Competition from the spread of four still numerous smaller species of otter that live in South America may also be important. *Message ends.*

D to 000. What other species of otter are also under significant threat?

000 to D. As well as the giant otter, the *marine otter* of South American coastlands is in danger, but many others, including the *Eurasian* and *North American otters* are also at risk as habitat destruction and water pollution take their toll.

Report ends: file **urgently**.

OPERATION MINERVA:

NAME □ **Snow Leopard**

ALIAS □ *Panthera uncia*

Also known as ounce. This name was once also applied to the lynx and the cheetah and is derived from the Latin word for lynx.

REPORTED SEEN □ Map ref P5

BACKGROUND □ Not much is known about this target. D is particularly fond of the cat family and considers this species to be the most glamorous and spectacular of all. It is a little smaller than a leopard, weighing 65-75 kg, with wonderfully long, dense fur of a smoky blue-grey colour tinged with pale yellow lightening to white on the underparts. The head and lower limbs display round black spots and the backs of the ears are black. The body markings are large, rather fuzzy rosettes among which are small dense black spots. The tail is relatively larger than that of a leopard, luxuriously furred and patterned with rings of dark rosettes. The pads of the paws are sensibly provided with furry

The most beautiful of all cats – a pair of snow leopards.

'snowshoes' which insulate them against the cold and also increase the weight-bearing area of the feet – useful when padding about in soft snow.

The *snow leopard* was first heard of by Europeans in 1761 when a French naturalist confused it with the cheetah by wrongly saying that it came from Persia where it was trained for hunting.

Other locations where it can be seen ☐

Many zoos including PORT LYMPNE, EDINBURGH and MARWELL (UK), BASLE (Switzerland), CHICAGO, CINCINNATTI (USA).

Estimated degree of survival threat ☐

Condition orange-red. Luckily it is breeding regularly in many zoos.

Special warning to investigating agents ☐

Take great care in approaching poachers of this animal – they are armed and known to react usually with violence.

Field report from 000 to D.

Top priority. Operation Minerva.
13 September. 09.45 hrs.
Have located the snow leopard with great difficulty and after much effort. It inhabits the high mountains of Afghanistan, and east to Siberia and Tibet, sometimes going up to the snowfields above 5,000 m. It is a shy, secretive cat adapted to life in a harsh environment. In winter it can be found at lower levels (2,000-3,000 m) in forests, where it follows its prey animals as they migrate down below the tree-line.

The snow leopard is a tough and highly agile cat that can make great leaps of up to 15 m. It is basically nocturnal, but frequently hunts by day and is particularly fond of the rugged but nimble ibex. It also takes wild sheep, musk deer, wild boar, small mammals like marmots and pikas, birds and, from time to time in the winter, domestic animals. Snow leopards are keen stalkers and setters of ambushes and they regularly patrol high points in the mountains from which they can sur-vey the terrain below. Like domestic cats, they love to roll about in the plant called catnip. They do not roar like lions but can purr, and like smaller felines they feed while in a crouched position. They possess a round eye pupil rather than a slit.

Usually solitary animals, snow leopards travel long distances throughout their immense territories, leaving typical feline 'markers' in the form of rocks and tree trunks sprayed with pungent urine, and also scratch marks on the ground. They shelter in a cleft in a rock or beneath an overhanging boulder, and in some areas take over the huge nests built by vultures in low trees. Pity the poor vulture that tries to evict a squatting snow leopard from its property!

Pregnancy in a female snow leopard lasts about 100 days, after which a litter of one to four young are born, normally in the spring or early summer. The mother delivers the cubs in a den, comfortably lined with her own moulted fur to a depth of 1-1.5 cm. The cubs weigh four to seven times as much as a newborn domestic kitten at birth. They open their eyes at about one week of age, first eat solids when they are one month old and are weaned at two to two and a half months. The young cubs stay with their mothers for about nine months.

The snow leopard's gorgeous coat led to it being hunted by man.

No snow leopard has ever attacked a human being unless severely provoked. In zoos they have lived for up to 15 years. *Message ends.*

D to 000. Please identify enemies of snow leopard.

000 to D. Re. snow leopard enemies.

1. Man. Unscrupulous hunters still covet this animal because of its beautiful coat and the fur trade continues to connive with them in order to supply vain and stupid women with snow leopard pelts. Although snow leopard hunting is illegal in most countries where it exists, poaching and trapping continues, particularly in Afghanistan and Kashmir. It is relatively easy to purchase snow leopard furs in Kashmir, a part of the animals' range where human persecution is particularly severe.

2. In some areas the natural prey of the snow leopard is disappearing as mountain pastures are developed for the grazing of domestic farm livestock. Consequently the snow leopard population simultaneously decreases. *Message ends.*

D to 000. Message received and understood. The fur trade in some countries is obviously still a prime offender. Hopefully governments will clamp down more firmly on exports and imports of snow leopard furs. If so-called 'fashionable' people refused to wear the fur, trade in it would cease and this magnificent cat of the remote Asian mountains might be safe from extinction.

Snow leopard cubs love to play just like domestic kittens.

A moment of extreme danger for a beautiful snow leopard.

OPERATION MINERVA: 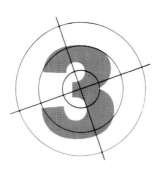 3

NAME □ **Rare Macaws**

ALIASES □ *Anodorhynchus hyacinthinus, Cyanopsitta spixii etc.*

REPORTED SEEN □ Map ref F9

BACKGROUND □ There are 328 species in the Psittacine family of birds which includes parrots, cockatoos and lories. One of them of course is the friendly budgerigar. The parrots of the New World first became known to Europeans in the fifteenth and sixteenth centuries when Spanish, Portuguese and English explorers began to penetrate South America, although Old World psittacines had been kept as talking pets in Greece since at least 400 BC. By the way, Shakespeare mentioned parrots in *The Merchant of Venice*; 'nature hath framed strange fellows in her time:

Forest destruction threatens rare parrots such as these hyacinthine macaws.

Some that will evermore peep through their eyes, And laugh like parrots at a bagpiper . . .'

Macaws are the largest and most spectacular members of the family. Like all parrots, they have the typical and familiar bill with the two curved mandibles, the upper of which is larger and more hooked than the lower one over which it fits. This bill is immensely powerful in macaws and can crack open Brazil nuts, inflict deep wounds on prying human fingers and also be employed as a useful climbing hook to assist the feet. The tongue is stubby, thick and muscular and contains a little bone. Note also the toes of parrots – unlike the arrangement in other birds, the two outer toes point backwards and the two inner ones point forwards. The foot of a parrot can not only be used for perching and climbing, but also as a most dextrous hand for grasping and manipulating things.

Incidentally, parrots are naturally either 'left-handed' or 'right-handed', and favour using one foot or the other, just like humans do with their hands. No other kind of bird is so 'handy' and skilled in using its feet as are parrots – not even the powerfully taloned eagles and hawks.

Macaws are vividly coloured birds, some of them bedecked in breathtaking

The useful grasping foot of a macaw.

multi-hued plumage. Although big, these strong birds are fast fliers.

Many species are endangered and some are on the verge of extinction. Your mission is to get at the facts about these very 'pretty pollies'.

Other locations where they can be seen □
Zoos, bird gardens and private aviaries.

Estimated degree of survival threat □
Condition green to red depending on species.

Field report from 000 to D.
Top priority. Operation Minerva.
4 October. 10.25 hrs.
There are many different species of macaw living in this part of the New World. They do *not* occur in the wild in Africa or Asia. Some are relatively small, like *Hahn's macaw*, which weighs about 165 g, while others are far bigger, the biggest being the *hyacinthine macaw* which tips the scales at up to 1.5 kg.

Like most other parrots of the region, macaws eat nuts, seeds and fruit, dwell in the trees of the rainforest, and nest in holes in tree trunks, either completely making the holes themselves or enlarging the holes made by other bird species. You can't tell a male from a female macaw just by looking at them – they appear identical (at least to the human eye!). Veterinary surgeons using a technique called endoscopy can find out which is which.

Female macaws lay two to four eggs, incubating them themselves for about 26 days, though the male does fuss about quite a lot in the nest during this time. It takes from three to three and a half months for the macaw chicks to grow their plumage (fledge) while they remain in the nest.

The kind of macaw kept as a pet, often seen in zoos and one of the most numerous in the wild, is the *blue and yellow*. It sports a bright blue back and wings with buttercup yellow underparts, and has a white face marked with black lines. Other

macaws you will surely see in aviaries are the *scarlet* and the *green-winged*.

But the central targets of my mission are the much rarer, more endangered macaws. It has been incredibly difficult to locate them. The largest of the macaws, the hyacinthine, possesses, not surprisingly, the biggest and strongest bill of any parrot. It could nip off your thumb with the greatest of ease. A marvellous lilac hyacinth colour, with bright yellow skin surrounding the eyes and the lower mandible, it is a stunning bird that lives in parts of the Brazilian, Paraguayan and Bolivian rainforest. Its numbers in the

A pair of hyacinthine macaws at their nest in the Brazilian rainforest.

145

The handsome scarlet macaw can often be seen in zoos and bird gardens.

wild are declining fast. Even rarer is the *Lear's macaw*, a smaller version of the hyacinthine, first discovered in 1978. Only one population of fewer than 100 birds is now thought to survive. Another parrot that resembles the Lear's, called the *glaucous macaw*, is probably already extinct.

Spix's macaw, the only macaw with a completely feathered head (all the others have bare faces) is blue with a grey head. Its home is the forest of north-eastern Brazil, but the number of birds in the wild is probably less than half a dozen – if that! Spix's macaw is without doubt the most endangered of all the parrots in South America. Very few are in captivity (about 20 in total worldwide) and there has been virtually no breeding so far. *Message ends.*

D to 000. Please identify enemies of the rare macaws.

000 to D. Re. Macaw enemies.

1. Man. Over the years birds have been taken from the wild in vast and irresponsible numbers for the pet trade and to supply zoos and aviaries. Many countries have now brought in laws to stop this

trade and there are international agreements to enforce them. Sadly some governments and customs services only pay lip-service to the protective legislation. Corruption, illegal poaching and smuggling continue to reduce the wild macaw populations, with many thousands of dollars being paid for specimens of the rarer species. Happily, lots of macaws are reproducing well in zoos and bird gardens, but some, such as the Spix's, are not, and may well soon disappear for ever.

2. Man. Destruction of the rainforest has eliminated the habitats of many parrot species including macaws such as the hyacinthine. While some parrots can adapt to life in the agricultural landscape that has replaced the Amazonian jungle in many areas, others, less versatile in their lifestyles, cannot and simply fade away. *Message ends.*

Fewer than a hundred of the very rare Lear's macaw now exist.

OPERATION MINERVA:

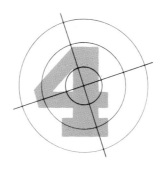

NAME ☐ **African Wild Ass**

ALIASES ☐ African wild donkey, *Equus africanus.*

REPORTED SEEN ☐ Map ref M6

BACKGROUND ☐ This mission is deadly serious, despite the fact that you might at first think the target is just another *donkey*. Everyone loves donkeys, but they are hardly rare or endangered (except in the sense that those rescued by donkey sanctuaries or the Horses and Ponies Protection Association are).

Ass is frequently used as an alternative name for donkey, and the animal you will seek in this phase of your mission is an ass and, further, the kind of ass from which the familiar domestic donkey is descended.

Ass, as you know only too well, is a common derogatory term for a stupid person. You may recall that Mr Bumble, the beadle in Charles Dickens' *Oliver Twist*, declared that 'the law is an ass – an idiot'. On the other hand, the ass or donkey has had its moments of great glory and importance; Jesus rode on one into Jerusalem on Palm Sunday; in Islam it is said that one of the ten animals to be admitted into heaven besides man is Balaam's ass, the one that spoke, mentioned in the Old

It's easy to see the relationship between the wild ass (here pictured) and the friendly donkey.

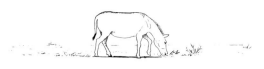

Testament of the Bible; and the ass was the symbol of one of the lost tribes of Israel.

Your target is no stubborn, stupid moke, much as it may look like one. It is in fact a fine, tough, intelligent and very rare species.

The *African wild ass* is bigger than most domestic donkeys, with long donkey-like ears, a grey body colour that shades to white on the underparts, white legs and a white muzzle. There is a thin black stripe along the back together with either a transverse stripe at the shoulder to make the cross design seen in ordinary donkeys or zebra-striped legs. The tail is tufted and the mane is thin, short and upright, 'punk-fashion'!

Other locations where it can be seen □
THE HAI BAR RESERVE in Israel, STUTTGART, WEST BERLIN (Germany), BASLE (Switzerland), SAN DIEGO (USA).

Estimated degree of survival threat □
Condition red.

The wild ass at home in typical terrain.

Field report from 000 to D.
Operation Minerva.
14 November. 09.00 hrs.
This has been my toughest assignment so far, entailing arduous journeys into the hottest, most arid places in the desert.

There are two races of African wild ass, the *Nubian* and the *Somali*. Both inhabit the most inhospitable terrain, where temperatures of 50°C (122°F) during the daytime are common. The asses live in herds of up to about ten animals, usually led by an old female, while the older males live separately. They somehow survive on what little desert vegetation they can find, grazing from dawn till mid-morning, resting during the heat of the day in the shade of a bush or a rocky hillock, and then feeding again from about 5 o'clock until sunset. During the night they sometimes trek long distances to water holes, but regularly go without for two days!

They are splendid beasts – masters of the desert. They run fast (up to at least 48 kmh) – and can spot trouble a long way off. Shy and cautious, they are quick to run for safety, but stop every now and then to look back and check whether they are being pursued. If cornered, they will

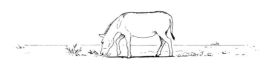

A young wild ass prepares to drink.

fight valiantly, kicking and biting hard and fast. No placid seaside, beach-plodding donkeys these!

Once, the wild ass was to be found across much of North Africa and there are ancient rock-face paintings of them still to be seen in Algeria. The wild ass has evolved, as you might expect, from the same ancestors as the horse. The details of their family tree are complex and still not completely worked out.

About 55 million years ago, in what are now called Europe and North America, but were then joined together in one land mass, a little dog-like animal moved through the forests, browsing on low shrubs. This was *Hyracotherium*, ancestor of the horses and also of the rhinoceroses and tapirs. Descended itself from forebears possessing the basic five toes per foot, it had already lost two outer toes on its hind feet and one inner toe on its fore feet, the remaining toes looking dog-like, with pads; there was no sign of hooves as yet. It had a short muzzle and a long tail held curved like a cat's. As the

149

Drought and civil war have been the principal enemies of the tough wild ass.

ages passed, the descendants of *Hyracotherium* split off into numerous branches of the family tree. The rhinos and tapirs went their way; the equine branch went theirs, discarding more toes so that they might concentrate on perfecting a single, highly modified toe on each foot, growing larger, developing teeth that were ideal for cropping and grinding grass, and acquiring large, efficient eyes.

By about one million years ago, all the surviving equine descendants of *Hyracotherium* had settled into four main groups; the horses, the asses, the half-asses and the zebras. These four groups were distributed in fairly specific parts of Africa, Europe and the Middle East, with almost no overlapping of the various groups. The zebras were purely Southern African and the half-asses (ancestors of the onager, kulan, kiang and djiggetai, and of the hemione which became extinct about one hundred years ago) were all Asiatic. The asses, from which donkeys later developed, were purely northern African and the horses (including ponies, which are simply horses under 14.2 hands

high) were inhabitants of Europe and Western Asia.

At the present time probably only 2-3,000 wild asses exist, though the military and political situation in Ethiopia may well have reduced that number drastically in recent years. *Message ends.*

D to 000. Please identify enemies of African wild ass.

000 to D. Re. wild ass enemies.
1. Man. Although supposedly protected in the areas where they exist, there is little doubt that the conditions of civil war in parts of Ethiopia and elsewhere in the wild asses' range, have resulted in the deaths of untold numbers of these animals.
2. The terrible drought which in recent years has resulted in so much human famine in Ethiopia, the Sudan etc., has also taken its toll of animals. *Message ends.*

150

OPERATION MINERVA: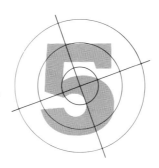

NAME □ **Komodo Dragon**

ALIASES □ Ora (the proper local name for this lizard), *Varanus komodoensis*.

REPORTED SEEN □ Map ref T6

BACKGROUND □ Rare, fascinating and dangerous, having been known to kill human beings on many occasions, this largest of living lizards lives on only Flores Komodo, Rintja and three other much smaller Indonesian islands in the Lesser Sunda group.

It can grow to over 3 m and specimens of perhaps as long as 5 m may have existed within living memory.

Depending on how full its stomach is, a 3 m long specimen can weigh between 100 and 250 kg, nothing compared with its even bigger relative that lived one million years ago and topped 2 tonnes!

An adult *Komodo dragon* has a stocky body and stout legs covered by scaly skin of an almost uniform grey colour whose texture reminds me of the outside of a lychee fruit, finely pimply rather than smooth and shiny like a snake. Young dragons are speckled and come in a variety of yellowish and greenish hues. The mouth carries a formidable array of backward-curved teeth designed for cutting flesh, and there is a bright yellow tongue that does the tasting, not

The flicking tongue of a dragon works much like that of a snake.

only of solids, but also, more importantly in such reptiles, of the air around it.

I have worked with these giant lizards and consider them to be more intelligent than most other reptiles; they really seem to watch you purposefully with their gleaming eyes. But be careful, 000, they can be very aggressive and may move surprisingly quickly. If you get into trouble, remember you're on your own!

Other locations where it can be seen □
Zoos at MADRID (Spain), ANTWERP (Belgium), SYDNEY (Australia), SAN DIEGO (USA).

Estimated degree of survival threat □
Condition yellow.

Field report from 000 to D.
Top priority. Operation Minerva.
3 January. 09.00 hrs.
The Komodo dragon is remarkable in having the smallest range of any of the large carnivores on this planet. In its island homes, some of which are very

Three Komodo dragons share a meal.

mountainous and volcanic, it mainly stays in the lowland, occasionally wandering as high as 2,000 m. A good swimmer, it can dive to 2 m and can cross small expanses of sea to reach other islands. Its typical environment is dry savannah land and the woodland that surrounds it. Woodland fires are often deliberately started by the human inhabitants for agricultural purposes, but the dragon itself doesn't seem much affected by them. It escapes by running off or retreating to its burrow.

Komodo dragons dig burrows in open hillsides or the banks of dry creek beds, but use them infrequently. The burrows are only a few metres deep and the lizards lie in them curled up like hairpins. They are active mainly by day, although they

A Komodo dragon in its lair.

A successful ambush on a young deer.

do occasionally hunt by the light of a full moon. Being big, they can store heat in their bodies and, although 'cold-blooded' are less dependent on surrounding temperature than smaller reptiles in order to keep active.

Of all their senses, scent is the most highly developed and important. Their power of sight enables them to recognise people up to about 6 m away and food at perhaps 50 m. They do not hear very well.

Among other species their enemies include the domestic dog, monkeys, wild boar, civet cats, birds of prey and some snakes which eat young dragons. More important is cannibalism among themselves. Hungry dragons – and they are often very hungry – eat their fellows, particularly smaller individuals. If a dragon can survive all that, he stands a chance of reaching the age of about 50 years.

Female dragons lay eggs in tree stumps or, more usually, holes excavated in the ground. One to 30 (usually about 15) eggs with soft, smooth, leathery shells (approximately 9 x 5 cm) are laid between July and early September. They hatch eight to eight and a half months later.

These giant lizards are essentially scavengers who search for dead animals using their sense of smell/taste. They compete with dogs, wild boar and birds for the corpses of deer and other animals. Only the dog dare challenge the dragon over ownership of a corpse – and then the dragon almost always has the last word. Sometimes the dragons will dig up human corpses from their graves and eat them!

The cutting teeth of this lizard and its great muscular power as it shakes its head to and fro after taking hold of an item of food, enable it to rip off enormous chunks of meat. It can crunch easily through bone and can swallow half a deer or the entire leg of a goat at one gulp. One 2.5 m long dragon was seen to swallow a 15 kg pig whole and three or four adult dragons can consume all of a large water buffalo in three to five days. When hungry they will eat small deer antlers or the horns of goats, and bones are no problem for them.

But these hungry reptiles are also predators who seek *living* prey. They ambush or trail deer, wild pigs and farm animals, probably aided by their keen sense of

Although unable to breathe fire, this dragon has a powerful bite.

smell. With large animals like buffaloes, they can inflict serious wounds which lead later to the death of the victim, an event patiently awaited by the lizard who tracks down the corpse with the aid of that ever-flicking tongue.

They lay their ambushes for wild boar at the side of the game trails regularly used by these animals, or at waterholes. There are many reports from villagers in the islands claiming that lizards are particularly attracted to mares, cattle and goats when they are heavily pregnant. They hang around in the hope of grabbing a newborn animal or, some scientists speculate, hope that their presence will trigger a miscarriage and that they can then carry off the foetus.

Komodo dragons frequently enter villages to take domestic animals and a number of attacks on human beings are reported, including the deaths of two tourists within recent years. *Message ends.*

D to 000. How many Komodo dragons do you estimate still to exist?

000 to D. Probably 4-5,000.

D to 000. Please identify enemies of the Komodo dragon.

000 to D. Re. Komodo dragon enemies.

The Indonesian government is enforcing protection of the Komodo dragons with much effort, but there remain:

1. Man. Illegal capture and killing. Sometimes villagers put poison in dead animals as bait for the lizards in order to get rid of them.
2. Starvation. Reduced availability of prey due to over-hunting of deer by man and changes in agricultural practice which have increased the numbers of farm livestock and further decreased the numbers of deer. Deer are the Komodo dragon's favourite prey.
3. Competition from feral (domestic animals gone back to the wild) dogs.
4. Uncontrolled burning of woodland reduces prey animals.

At present the position of the Komodo dragon is stable, but it remains highly vulnerable. *Message ends.*

OPERATION MINERVA:

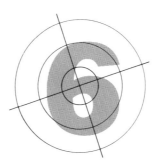

NAME □ Okapi

ALIAS □ *Okapia johnstoni*

REPORTED SEEN □ Map ref L7

BACKGROUND □ Your target in this instance is a most mysterious and elusive character. Western scientists first heard of its existence in 1901, when a British explorer, Johnstone, went in search of the horse-like animal that the pigmy people called 'okapi'. He found it living in the deep rainforest. A zoologist who examined the first bits of skin of the animal that were sent back to London, thought it was a new species of zebra and gave it the Latin name *Equus* (horse) *johnstoni*.

The shy okapi is the giraffe's closest living relative.

A remarkable and attractive creature, the *okapi* is the giraffe's closest living relative, though I find it to be more placid by nature than the latter. It wears a luxurious velvety chocolate-coloured coat of short hair with a gleaming sheen. The males have skin-covered peg-like 'horns' similar to those of giraffes and the head is rather giraffe-shaped, as is the neck, though much shorter in length. Again, like the giraffe, the okapi's 'fang' (canine) teeth are splayed out into lobes designed to strip the leaves off shoots when browsing, the tongue is long, extendible and dark grey, for grasping and plucking foliage, and, though there is none of the patched skin decoration of the giraffe, there are creamy coloured stripes on the legs and buttocks. Altogether the skin coloration and patterning is perfect camouflage for life in deep jungle conditions. The animals have large mobile ears and large dark eyes, both employed effectively in detecting approaching danger. Bull okapis stand about 1.7 m high and weigh up to 300 kg. The cows are a little bigger than the bulls.

Basically we know very little about the ways of the okapi in its native haunts – not surprising in view of the difficulty of studying it in the gloom of the dense forest. We don't even know how threatened it is. Some scientists

The remarkably long tongue of the okapi is great for cleaning the face.

The okapi's longish neck enables it to browse on trees.

think it is in danger, but without being in risk of imminent extinction. Go to it, 000 (don't forget to have your yellow fever vaccination and take your anti-malaria pills).

Other locations where it can be seen □
Zoos in BRISTOL (UK), BASLE (Switzerland), CHICAGO, COLORADO and DALLAS (USA).

Estimated degree of survival threat □
Condition yellow.

D to 000. *2 February. 09.00 hrs*. Am still awaiting your report, now one month overdue.

000 to D. *Top priority. Operation Minerva. 4 February. 22.00 hrs.*
Have been laid up with typhoid fever.

Foolishly ate some soft fruit washed in village well water. Had my camera stolen while I was down with the fever.

Field report from 000 to D.
After many days hacking through almost impenetrable jungle and making enquiries at innumerable villages I have located the target here in Zaire.

Okapis inhabit relatively discrete areas of remote jungle, usually of secondary tree growth, with one or two animals living solitary lives per square kilometre of territory. They browse on low bushes of all kinds, taking young shoots, leaves and fruit. They have their own preferred pathways through the bush linking feeding zones, and mark their 'property' by leaving secretions on the ground from glands between their toes (giraffes do not possess these) and by urinating on bushes and trees. Probably each territory is the domain of a particular male okapi with females moving from one territory to another.

Like giraffes, okapis can live for over 30 years. Normally silent animals except when tending their young, the females call during the mating period which lasts about one month. Male okapis indulge in courtship displays that include head tossing, lip-curling and flicking of the legs. Sometimes two bulls will do battle over a female, either in ritual form, 'necking' like giraffe bulls do by pressing their necks together in a contest of strength, or more seriously by actually charging and butting one another.

Pregnancy in the female okapi lasts just over 14½ months after which a single calf is born, usually in the rainy season. Curiously, and I think uniquely among mammals, the calf does not have its first bowel movement until 10-14 days after birth – this appears quite normal and harmless. Unlike the adults, the calf possesses a narrow stiff black mane and relatively thicker legs and smaller head and neck. It stays hidden in the undergrowth for the first month of its life, relying on its camouflage to hide it from important pre-

dators such as the leopard, and exchanging low bleating or whistling sounds with its mother from time to time. If a leopard does attack a calf, the parent will attempt to drive it off with powerful kicks of the legs.

Recently some scientists have suggested that the okapi may not be as closely related to the giraffe as has been generally thought, and that its nearest 'kith and kin' may be the *nilgai*, the large 'horse antelopes' that live in India and do look a bit okapi-like to me. *Message ends.*

D to 000. How many okapi do you estimate still to exist?

000 to D. Number totally unknown. There may be hundreds or perhaps a few thousand.

The beautiful okapi is well camouflaged for the deep jungle.

D to 000. Please identify enemies of the okapi.

000 to D. Re. okapi enemies.

1. Man, the hunter. Although the okapi has been protected by law since 1933 in this country, it is extremely difficult, because of the terrain, to prevent illegal hunting. For thousands of years pygmies who also live in this region have hunted okapis as part of their unending struggle to survive in the jungle, and they pose no threat to the survival of the species. It is men from outside, the greedy commercial poachers, killing the okapi to obtain its much valued meat, who are the true enemy.

D to 000. Report received. The Organisation will expect you to reimburse it for the loss of one camera. *Message ends.*

OPERATION MINERVA:

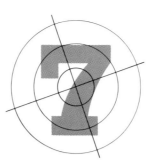

NAME □ Cuban Crocodile

ALIASES □ *Crocodylus rhombifer,*Cocodrilo de Cuba.

REPORTED SEEN □ Map ref E6

BACKGROUND □ **DANGER.**
DANGER. The target is the rarest of all crocodilians, that ancient family of reptiles that includes crocodiles, alligators, ghavials and caimans – six of which are extremely dangerous man-eaters!

There are 25 species of crocodilian ranging in size from the 1 m long *Congo dwarf crocodile* to the fiercesome *saltwater crocodile*, perhaps the most dangerous of the lot, which can reach 6 and perhaps even 9 m in length.

Like all reptiles, crocodiles are 'cold-blooded' – their bodies are the same temperature as that of their immediate environment. They have heavily scaled skins and a muscular tail that is flattened from side to side and which is 'skulled' to push the animal through the water, while the limbs are tucked into the body. On land they can raise themselves up on their legs, with their body held well off the ground, and they can run quite fast. When they are not in the rivers, sluggish streams and lakes (and in the case of the saltwater crocodile, sometimes the sea) where they live, they may be found hauled out on sand-bars and banks, basking in the sunshine with their huge jaws gaping widely – not to catch things, but in order to lose excess heat. They don't mind when birds enter their open mouths to pick bits of food from between their teeth. I suppose they regard them as useful living toothbrushes!

A crocodile with its living toothpick.

There are many legends about the crocodile. The ancient Egyptians worshipped them as divine and made mummies of their dead bodies. They believed that the crocodile was the only animal with eyes covered by a thin transparent membrane (not true), that allowed it to see without being seen – something that surely only a god could do.

You will know why we refer to 'crocodile tears' – false displays of sadness. It was believed that crocodiles shed tears over their prey while in the

The saltwater crocodile is probably the most dangerous of all crocodiles.

act of devouring it. Shakespeare says in *Henry VI*, 'as the mournful crocodile, with sorrow snares relenting passengers'. Funnily enough, there may be a grain of truth in this. When a croc has torn a large chunk of flesh off its victim and is swallowing it, pressure is exerted on the rather thin and flexible roof of the back of the reptile's mouth. This squeezes the tear glands which lie just above so that tears well up into the

eyelids and spill over. Crocodile tears, like those of humans, contain an antiseptic chemical which protects the eye from infection, particularly valuable to creatures who live in muddy water.

Another legend refers to crocodiles eating their young. This may arise from the fact that when the baby crocodiles hatch, their mother takes them very gently into her jaws and shakes them down into the pouched floor of her mouth. Then she carries them down to the water and sometimes swims with a mouthful of a dozen or more snappy little youngsters peeping out from between her teeth.

Other locations where it can be seen □
Zoos in HAVANA (Cuba) and elsewhere.

Estimated degree of survival threat □
Orange-red.

From the British Ambassador, Havana, to **D**. Top Security Code. Channel 86 scrambled telex. 23 March. 11.04 hrs. My staff have visited one of your field operatives detained by Cuban Intelligence Service. What is going on? My intelligence officer knows nothing of any current operations involving your section. Out.

D to British Ambassador, Havana. 23 March. 15.00 hrs. TOP SECURITY CODE. Channel 86 scrambled telex. Many apologies. Will explain next time you are back in UK when we can have a drink. Out.

One of the differences between a crocodile and an alligator is the way the fourth lower tooth fits into the lower jaw.

Field report from 000 to D.
Top Priority. Operation Minverva.
28 March. 06.15 hrs.
Had a spot of trouble when exploring the swampland of Cienaga de Zapata in central Cuba, a small area which is the last refuge of the *Cuban crocodile* in the wild. I was arrested by a patrol of Cuban soldiers and interrogated for six days. They thought I was a spy and refused to believe that The Organisation is purely concerned with endangered animals. Eventually the guy in charge said, 'So you claim to be nothing more than a keen biologist, *not* a spy – if that's the truth, prove it! Tell me – what is the main difference between a crocodile and an alligator?'

Was I relieved! Quick as a flash I told him – the fourth tooth on the lower jaw of an alligator fits neatly into a pit formed for it in the upper jaw, not into a notch at the side of the jaw as in crocodiles. Also, an alligator head is broader and shorter than a croc's and it doesn't have the jagged fringe that you'll find on the hind legs and feet of a crocodile. He checked with some professor and then I was free! Here is my delayed field report:

The Cuban crocodile can now only be found in this one small swamp. Although not one of the biggest crocodilians, it can grow up to around 4 m long and is very stocky and muscular, with teeth that are tilted outwards. It is undoubtedly the most bad tempered and aggressive species, and in the past, when it was more numerous, has attacked and killed human beings on occasion. But it has nothing like the reputation of other crocodiles such as the saltwater crocodile that probably kills 2-3,000 people per year or

Alligator

Crocodile

A surprisingly good mother, a female Nile crocodile carries her babies gently in her mouth.

the *Nile crocodile* which kills about 1,000 and has been known to take on horses and even big rhinoceroses which were drinking at the water's edge.

Crocodiles stalk their prey, watching with those cold eyes that protrude just above the water surface, swimming in stealthily and then suddenly launching an attack. The victim is seized – a croc's bite is 60 times stronger than that of the strongest man – and with furious twisting and shaking movements of its body, the reptile takes its prey down through the water. More twisting and spinning of its body tears limbs or large chunks of flesh

from the unfortunate victim – a croc's teeth are for grabbing and holding, not slicing and chewing. Sometimes crocodiles put bodies into underwater 'larders', small caves or beneath boulders, for a few days where decomposition will soften them and make them easier to dismember. Normally, however, Cuban crocodiles eat fish, birds and any small mammals they can catch.

Like all crocodiles and alligators, Cuban crocodiles reproduce by laying eggs. The eggs are white and oval, rather like goose eggs, and they are laid in a mound of rotting vegetation where they incubate by the heat of fermentation of the 'compost'. The mother guards the nest from intruders, and scratches away the

vegetation covering the eggs when the youngsters call to her, making hiccup-like cries from within the egg, when they are ready to hatch! The babies cut their way out of the tough egg-shell by means of an 'egg-tooth' which they have on the tip of their snout, but which is lost soon after birth. Growth in crocodiles depends on environmental temperature and the amount of available food, but is usually about 0.3 m per year for the first few years and more slowly after that. They can live to a great age – some experts think as much as 200 years. *Message ends.*

D to 000. How many Cuban crocodiles do you estimate still to exist?

000 to D. A few hundred. Luckily the Cuban government has declared the swamp a sanctuary and the animals are effectively protected.

D to 000. Please identify enemies of the crocodile.

The closest living relatives of the dinosaur, a group of Cuban crocodiles bask in the sun.

000 to D. Re. crocodile enemies.

1. Man. The Cuban crocodile is probably safe, provided the swampland remains a sanctuary and is not drained in the future for agricultural or other development. In the past it was severely overhunted for its skin to make fancy leather goods. Other species of crocodile still suffer from hunters – crocodile skins continue to fetch very high prices. Controlled hunting and the setting up of crocodile farms can help to conserve these fascinating animals in the wild, but the numbers of some once-plentiful crocodiles are dropping steadily. No longer is the Nile crocodile to be found in Egypt – you remember that verse in *Alice in Wonderland* –

'How doth the little crocodile
Improve his shining tail,
And pour the waters of the Nile,
On every golden scale!'

OPERATION MINERVA:

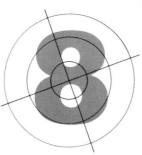

NAME □ African Hunting Dog

ALIASES □ African wild dog, Cape hunting dog, painted dog, tri-coloured dog.

REPORTED SEEN □ Map ref M9

BACKGROUND □ This is another mission that you should not under-estimate, 000. A dog, yes, but an increasingly endangered species of dog and one that could easily soon become extinct. Normally, when folk talk of rare dogs, they are referring to *unusual breeds* of domestic dog like the Caes de Agua, the Loewchen or the Glen of Imaal, pedigree aristocrats that you rarely see at a small dog show alongside the popular labradors, German shepherds and poodles. And among wild dogs there are some little-known and rarely seen species such as the *bush dog* of South America and the *dhole* of Asia, though the most threatened species is the *hunting dog*, a native of Africa.

This dog is certainly the most carnivorous of all the canine family and typifies the cooperative, social, versatile and intelligent character that made the dogs such an evolutionary success. Where cats are highly specialised, often solitary, self-reliant hunters, dogs are animals of the pack, adaptable and not over-specialised in any aspect – qualities that have enabled them to spread over the planet to a great extent.

Both dogs and cats originated about 60 million years ago from a small, weasel-like animal with a long, flexible body, long tail and short legs, that lived in

Hunting dogs attack a gnu.

You can see why the hunting dog is sometimes called the 'painted' dog.

forests. Its name was *Miacis*.

The canid family of dogs, wolves, foxes, coyotes and jackals (perhaps the hunting dog's closest relatives) all have one thing in common – long, narrow heads with long jaws and plentiful teeth. The cheek teeth are adapted partly for slicing and partly for grinding and can efficiently handle both meat and vegetable foods. The African hunting dog's teeth emphasise the slicing functions and indeed it eats virtually nothing but raw meat.

Hunting dogs are rangy animals standing about as high as a pointer or Irish setter and weighing up to 35 kg. They have a very short, dark coat that bears irregular yellow, orange and white blotches in a pattern which is unique to each individual. The legs are long and greyhound-like and the tail ends in a bush tipped with white. The ears are large and rounded, helping to keep the dog cool by radiating heat.

Other locations where it can be seen □
Zoos at PORT LYMPNE (UK) and in USA.

Estimated degree of survival threat □
Red.

Field report from 000 to D.
Top priority. Operation Minerva.
11 April. 14.45 hrs.
My landrover was overturned by a charging rhino this morning and as a result my

radio is out of action. This report comes to you courtesy of the British High Commission radio room in the capital.

It was not easy to locate the target species, undoubtedly because they are greatly reduced in numbers, often with no more than one pack per 2,000 sq. km of countryside.

Miacis, ancestor of the dog family, lived many millions of years ago.

The hunting dogs form packs of 2-32 animals with an average of about a dozen, though packs of up to 50 have been recorded. Long ago packs perhaps numbered hundreds. They travel longer distances than wolves, covering up to 50 km a day over their hunting territory which may be perhaps 40 sq. km in area when game is plentiful, but expand to 200 sq. km when it is scarce.

The pack does everything together — hunting, travelling and resting, and each individual works for the common good. As hunters, they do not depend on stalking, ambushing or the single-handed fast, but brief, attack, like the tiger or leopard. The hunting dog strategy is one of cooperation and stamina.

The dogs can keep up a chase for long distances. First one member of the pack will lead in pursuing the prey, and then, as he begins to flag, another will move up to the front. The chase continues relentlessly with the dogs being able to keep going at 48 kmh for over 5 km and, if necessary, accelerating for short bursts up to 55 kmh. They hunt by sight, recognising each of their comrades by their individual coat patterns, and signalling with their large, mobile ears. Using such hunting methods, they can bring down much larger animals like zebras and eland, and on occasion they have been known to tire out and kill a lone lion. Their main prey are small antelopes and gazelle, particularly Thomson's gazelle, and they also catch rodents and other small mammals.

Hunting dog packs have an unusual social structure with separate 'pecking orders' of males and females, each ruled

A pack of hunting dogs chase a gazelle.

Hunting dogs working together will sometimes take on a solitary lion.

by one top dog – a 'king' and a 'queen'. All of the males, and likewise the females, are related to one another; but only the 'queen' is related to any of the males. The 'queen' alone is allowed to breed and raise a litter of pups. Other females' litters are normally killed by the 'queen'. Males born and allowed to survive stay with the pack for their entire lives – generally shorter than those of domestic dogs at about ten years. Females stay until they are between one and two and a half years of age and then leave as a group to join a separate pack.

The packs look after the lucky pups very thoughtfully, staying near the den where they are born until they are old enough at about three months to go a-roaming with the adults. When they are weaned at nine to ten weeks, the pups are protected and supplied with food by members of the pack as a whole. *Message ends.*

D to 000. I await your detailed explanation of your squabble with the rhino with much interest when you return. How many African hunting dogs do you estimate still to exist?

000 to D. Probably only a few thousand now – a dramatic reduction in recent years. Once they were to be found almost everywhere in the continent. Now many packs are isolated.

D to 000. Please identify enemies of the African hunting dog.

000 to D. Re. African hunting dog enemies.

1. Man. (a) By persecuting the dogs themselves.
   (b) Diminishing habitat due to the expansion of human populations and activities.
2. Drastic reduction in the numbers of some prey animals such as springbok from various causes, in southern Africa.
3. Serious epidemics of the disease which domestic dogs are vaccinated against – distemper.

In some areas where they still exist they have legal protection and some packs do live in national parks like the Serengeti.

OPERATION MINERVA: 9

NAME □ **Lemurs**

ALIASES □ Various local and scientific names.

REPORTED SEEN □ Map ref N9

BACKGROUND □ The Romans gave the name *lemur* to the spirits of the dead and believed there were two kinds, the good ones, *lares*, and the terrifyingly bad ones, *larvae*. The delightful animals that have inherited the name *lemur* were regarded as mysterious, ghost-like creatures by the first humans with whom they came into contact, both natives and early European explorers of their island home.

There are accounts of men with dog's heads in many civilisations. Marco Polo said that these people lived on the Andaman Islands in the Indian Ocean. In Byzantine art, St Christopher is often depicted with a canine head and the legend runs that the saint was so uncommonly handsome that he prayed

One of the most comical sights in nature, an indri lemur walking along.

167

A ring-tailed lemur leaping through the trees.

to God to give him a dog's head to stop the girls pursuing him. The medieval Sir John Mandeville wrote of dog-men inhabiting an island which he called Macumera. Very possibly he was referring to the place where you will seek your target, for there is one species of lemur, the large *indri*, which does possess a rather dog-like head and a very human-like body.

Lemurs, of course, are not dogs, but primates like you and me. They are so called 'lower primates', being less advanced than man, the three great apes and monkeys. The lower primates have smaller brains in proportion to their body size, and longer snouts on their faces. They possess a better sense of smell, but do not have the ability to see a broad spectrum of colours, like we more advanced primates.

All species of lemur – there are at present 23, including one discovered only in 1987 – live in the same large

island of Madagascar and nowhere else. They range in size from one of the smallest of all primates, the *grey lesser mouse lemur* that weighs a mere 45-80 g and is 27-30 cm long, including the tail, to the 10 kg indri. One of the rarest of all primates is the *hairy-eared dwarf lemur*, the first live specimen of which was found just over 20 years ago.

Lemurs are furry creatures with long, often bushy tails and fore limbs (arms) that are distinctly shorter than the hind limbs (legs). The coat colours of different species are varied – some being more or less monochrome grey or brown, while others sport zones of two contrasting colours, black and white or black and red, for example. All have black muzzles with a damp nosepad, and an array of sensitive whiskers.

Lemurs are great sniffers and smellers, using scent produced by scent glands in their skin to communicate with one another. Other methods of communication between these animals are visual and vocal. Some have striking

signal designs on their body, like the *ring-tailed lemur* with distinct black and grey-white bands on its tail, and they can utter a variety of calls.

Other locations where they can be seen □
Many zoos including LONDON, TWYCROSS, EDINBURGH, (UK) SAN DIEGO, WASHINGTON, (USA) etc.

Estimated degree of survival threat □
Yellow to red.

Field report from 000 to D.
Top priority. Operation Minerva.
16 May. 06.00 hrs.
Please forgive any garbling of this report. Having difficulty speaking after being stung on lower lip by a very aggressive African hornet.

Have located various species of the target animal, but some are exceedingly rare and difficult to track down, particularly the nocturnal kinds. Once there were many more species of lemur on the island, including one as big as an orang-outang. The evolution of lemurs is a fascinating story; it seems that their ancestors came to the island, perhaps on mats of floating vegetation, some 50 million years ago. Separated from their fellows on the huge continent nearby, they then evolved in their own unique way. But then, of course, it had to happen! Man the hunter arrived on the island. He started to establish settlements there about 2,000 years ago. The rich collection of lemurs, some rather like koala bears, others baboon-like and still others rather gibbonish, soon started to suffer. Man's fire destroyed the forest habitat and his domestic animals competed with and harassed the lemurs. He also considered them an excellent source of food.

Surviving lemurs are forest-dwellers with only the ring-tailed lemur (the sort most commonly seen in zoos) spending much time on the ground. All are vegetarians who pick leaves, young shoots and fruits. One, the *mongoose lemur*, also gathers sweet nectar from flowers; the dwarf and mouse lemurs eat lots of insects; and the dwarf lemurs also collect gum (not bubble-gum!) from trees.

Some species are active during the day, others at night, and still others keep busy in spells around the clock. The nocturnal types have large eyes with a light-gathering 'mirror' of cells containing shiny crystals set behind the retina of their eyes.

Lemur society varies according to the species. Some lead fairly solitary lives (i.e. the *sportive lemur*), others live as strongly-bonded pairs together with their offspring (i.e. the mongoose lemur) and many form bigger groups of 5-35 animals (i.e. the ring-tailed lemur).

The tiniest lemurs are the ones we know least about. They are totally tree-

The charming mongoose lemur.

The strange and persecuted aye-aye.

dwelling, night workers who often make nests out of leaves.

The biggest lemurs are day-workers and to me the most fascinating is the indri. It is called 'babakoto' in the local language and in the old legends of the island is said to be man's ancestor. It often sits in a posture rather like that of a human being, and when it hops along the ground with its arms held outstretched to the sides or above its head, with the body tilted backwards and its tummy thrust forwards, it does make a comic impersonation of a rather tipsy ballet dancer or high-wire artiste.

The oddest of all the lemur group is the solitary and nocturnal *aye-aye*. This strange creature has a thick brown coat sprinkled with white hairs, big ears, long front teeth and a very long middle finger on each hand. It feeds on hard-shelled fruits such as coconut – that's why it needs the long teeth to deal with the shell and the long finger to scoop out the contents! The large ears are useful for listening out for the grubs which it also loves to eat, as they squirm about under the tree bark.

The aye-aye is almost extinct, not just because of the destruction of its habitat, but also because local people, noting its strange witch-like finger, vampirish teeth and overall weird appearance, consider it a devilish beast and kill it. *Message ends.*

D to 000. Please identify enemies of the lemur.

000 to D. Re. enemies of the lemur.

1. Man. Habitat destruction to produce timber and land for agriculture. Some species are trapped and shot for eating. Some of the more specialised species like the *gentle lemur*, which depend on supplies of bamboo, are at more imminent risk than others which have more flexible diets and lifestyle. There are protected areas on the island, but they cover only a very small part of the total lemur territory. It is to be hoped that such zones can be increased in size and number and that the well thought out management schemes can be expanded.

OPERATION MINERVA: 10

NAME ☐ **Gorilla**

ALIAS ☐ *Gorilla gorilla*

REPORTED SEEN ☐ Map ref L7

BACKGROUND ☐ In about 500 BC, the Carthaginian navigator, Hanno, wrote of his voyage of exploration to the west coast of Africa. He reported the existence there of an animal allegedly called 'gorilla' by the natives and that name was eventually adopted by scientists in Europe in the mid-nineteenth century.

The largest of the three anthropoid (man-like) apes, the *gorilla* had, until recently the undeserved reputation of a wild thug or ruffian of the jungle. The 1933 film *King Kong*, based on a novel by Edgar Wallace, in which a giant gorilla terrorises the city of New York, contributed to the myth of the animals' aggressiveness. What nonsense!

Although without doubt a mighty, muscle-rippling beast that can tip the scales at up to 275 kg (Phil, a gorilla at

Gorillas are now seriously threatened.

171

St Louis Zoo, who died in 1958, was claimed to have weighed a spectacular 352 kg!), standing taller than most men at a little over 2 m and boasting a chest measurement of 170 cm, an arm span of 2.7 m and 63 cm biceps, the gorilla is in fact a shy, peaceable and delightful character. In my experience, he is far less dangerous than the mercurial and immensely strong adult chimpanzee.

Of all the targets in your current mission, the gorilla is the one which, in my view, is most likely to vanish from its old haunts during our lifetime.

Gorillas are heavily built apes, closely related to chimpanzees, but much bigger and with different bodily proportions. A big crest of bone running from back to front along the top of the skull is particularly pronounced in male gorillas and produces the high head so distinctive of these animals. Gorillas have much smaller ears than chimps and nostrils which are surrounded by broad ridges of hairless, shiny skin.

There are three races of gorilla. The *mountain gorilla* is the largest of the three and, as its name suggests, lives in tropical forests up to an altitude of about 3,800 m. Its hair is rather longer than the others and is black with a silvery 'saddle' on the back of mature males.

The *Eastern lowland gorilla* is similar to the mountain gorilla but with shorter hair and somewhat longer arms.

The *Western lowland gorilla* has a coat of greyish-brown and the silvery saddle of the male extends the buttocks and upper thighs.

Other locations where they can be seen □
Many zoos such as HOWLETT'S, CHESSINGTON, LONDON (UK), SAN DIEGO (USA), etc.

Estimated degree of survival threat □
Red. Particularly the mountain gorilla.

Field report from 000 to D.
Top priority. Operation Minerva.
2 July. 13.00 hrs.
I am exhausted! The rainforest is incredibly hard going and I have been plagued by mosquitoes as big as elephants. Nevertheless, true to the traditions of The Organisation, I have achieved my objectives. The targets have been located.

The Western lowland gorilla lives in the region of map ref L10 while the Eastern lowland and mountain races inhabit bamboo and higher altitude rainforests about 1,000 km to the east at map ref N8.

Gorillas are strict vegetarians feeding on a variety of leaves, shoots, herbs and some fruit. Not for them the occasional meat meal like the chimpanzees who will kill and devour monkeys and birds. They

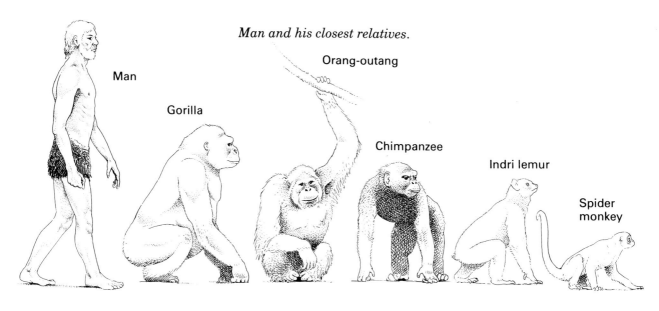

Man and his closest relatives.

Man

Gorilla

Orang-outang

Chimpanzee

Indri lemur

Spider monkey

Mum's back is the perfect spot for a baby gorilla's nap.

form permanent groups of about a dozen animals including youngsters, with a big male as leader. Sometimes groups of 30 or more have been recorded.

The gorillas are active by day and build nests in trees or lower vegetation at night by pulling branches and leaves down into a rough hammock. They feed in the morning, rest during the greatest heat in the middle of the day, and then feed again during the late afternoon. Each day the troop travels a short distance of 0.5-1 km within their territories which cover an area of 5-30 sq. km. Where gorillas live there is plenty of food and thus they do not need to travel far to gather their meals, and although one can speak of territories belonging to particular gorilla troops, there is no defence of these areas, and much overlapping of territories occurs without outbreaks of warfare or even proprietorial indignation.

Baby gorillas are born at any time of the year after a pregnancy of 251-289 days. They weigh about 2 kg at birth. They begin to crawl at about two months of age and can walk at about seven to ten

months. They wean when they are around two and a half years old. Sadly – but that is nature's way – about one in three young gorillas don't reach their third birthday.

Gorillas are not aggressive and don't fight or indulge in inter-tribal battles like chimpanzees. Sometimes a leading male gorilla will drive off another male with awesome-looking displays of bellicose behaviour – charging, chest-beating and roaring – but it's almost always theatre, an impressive display of bluff, and it seldom gets serious.

The same applies to gorilla/human encounters. You might be subjected to the showy bluff that I've just mentioned, but it is very rare indeed for a gorilla physically to harm a human being unless it feels that its family group is in some way being threatened. We have little to fear from gorillas; they have much to fear from us. *Message ends.*

D to 000. How many gorillas do you estimate still to exist?

000 to D. Perhaps about 11,000, of which fewer than 300 are mountain gorillas.

D to 000. Please identify enemies of the gorilla.

000 to D. Re. Gorilla enemies.

1. Man. The destruction of habitat. Forest is being cleared to provide timber and make way for agriculture, including domestic livestock.
2. Man. Gorillas are killed by the local population because they sometimes raid crops such as plantations of bananas.
3. Man. Some people kill gorillas to eat them. I have located restaurants in towns such as Libreville where gorilla steaks are on the menu!

The threatening display of a gorilla is more for show than for real.